Anger Management for Beginners

Anger Management for Beginners

Giles Coren

A Self-Help Course in 70 Lessons

HODDER

First published in Great Britain in 2010 by Hodder & Stoughton
An Hachette UK company

First published in paperback in 2010

1

Copyright © Giles Coren 2010

The right of Giles Coren to be identified as the Author of the Work has been
asserted by him in accordance with the Copyright, Designs and Patents Act 1988.

A CIP catalogue record for this title is available from the British Library.

ISBN 978 1 444 70688 8

Typeset in MT Sabon by Hewer Text UK Ltd, Edinburgh

Printed and bound by Clays Ltd, St Ives plc

Hodder & Stoughton policy is to use papers that are natural, renewable
and recyclable products and made from wood grown in sustainable forests.
The logging and manufacturing processes are expected to conform to the
environmental regulations of the country of origin.

Hodder & Stoughton Ltd
338 Euston Road
London NW1 3BH

www.hodder.co.uk

For Esther

Contents

e-Rage

'Don't make me angry. You wouldn't like me when I'm angry . . .'
Dr Bruce Banner – aka, The Hulk

On the morning of Saturday 5 April 2008, I woke up full of the joys of spring. I threw open the curtains of my north London bedroom and all but greeted the blue sky and tinkling buds with a burst of song. While my girlfriend set about boiling the kettle for tea and digging in the fridge for a suitably weekendy breakfast (oh, please let there be sausages), I shuffled into a pair of jeans and a holey old jumper and headed off down the road, as I do each morning, to buy the papers.

I waved to a couple of neighbours, nodded to a happy drunk on the traffic island as I crossed the main road at the bottom of my quiet residential street, and then ducked into the newsagent to pick up, as I always do, *The Times*, *The Guardian* and whichever red top has the nakedest girl on the front.

On the way back up my road I stopped to stroke at least two cats, and to be buoyed by the warm growl as they wound round my calves. I chatted to Bill, the retired sparks who still lives next door to my old flat across the road, and helped Millicent, from number 46, to load her son onto his seat at the back of her bicycle.

When I walked through my front door, ten minutes after I had left, the house smelled of coffee and the juices of a good sausage, just beginning to caramelise on the base of an enamelled pan.

I poured myself a coffee at the kitchen table, had a quick ogle at Lindsay Lohan on the front of the *Mirror*, tossed *The Guardian* onto a windowsill (nobody in our house reads it – we just get it in case vegans arrive unexpectedly for lunch and need something to read on the loo), and cracked open *The Times* for a read of my favourite columnist, me.

It's what I love best about Saturdays, reading myself. Not in a smug or arrogant way (although I may not be the best judge of that). Nor because I think I am a better writer than any of the others, or funnier or more incisive. It's just that, of all columnists, I am the one who most reliably addresses the exact issues about which I care most. My opinion column in the Comment pages always chimes exactly with what I have been thinking about the week's news myself. And the restaurant review always seems, by some miracle, to be of somewhere I have recently been – so that I am in a great position to compare my own memories with the view of the critic.

And it was to my restaurant review that I turned first, wrenching open the plastic bag, watching the pitter-patter of flyers, ads and CD giveaways falling to the floor like multi-coloured rain, and then flicking hurriedly through the fresh, shiny pages to my review.

Café Boheme, bla bla bla, long boring intro as usual, sort of wish I had done it different but a bit late now, now for the food, set up final (excellent) joke about getting a nosh in Soho and . . . wait. What's this? Oh no.

And my morning fell apart.

Upstairs I rushed to my computer, hit the power button (generally the computer stays off all weekend, it's pretty much a golden rule), and then paced the floor of my study waiting for it to fire up – Come on! Come on! Suddenly the scent of coffee was gone from my nostrils and all I could smell was shit and sulphur, hellfire and brimstone.

Jesus H. Christ, heads will roll for this.

HEADS WILL FUCKING ROLL!!!

The screen flickered into life, I put in the addresses of as many *Times* Magazine sub-editorial staff as I could think of, and began to type, fast and hard and without looking back.

Chaps, [I wrote, because I wanted to start gently]

I am mightily pissed off. I have addressed this to Owen, Amanda and Ben because I don't know who i am supposed to be pissed off with (i'm assuming owen, but i filed to amanda and ben so it's only fair), and also to Tony, who wasn't here - if he had been I'm guessing it wouldn't have happened. [Tony is my editor – I would never speak to him like this.]

I don't really like people tinkering with my copy for the sake of tinkering. I do not enjoy the suggestion that you have a better ear or eye for how I want my words to read than I do. Owen, we discussed your turning three of my long sentences into six short ones in a single piece, and how that wasn't going to happen anymore, so I'm really hoping it wasn't you that fucked up my review on saturday. [Looking at it now I hate myself for sounding so pompous – 'we discussed . . .' – but the frothing, badly punctuated sentences only remind me how much I actually wanted to kill this man, genuinely wanted to hit him with a brick, and hit him and hit him and hit him until he died, and his mother wept, and his whole street turned out to watch a coffin covered with white flowers woven into the word 'Owen' proceed slowly towards the cemetery on the back of a horse-drawn hearse.]

It was the final sentence. Final sentences are very, very important. A piece builds to them, they are the little jingle that the reader takes with him into the weekend. [That was going to come back and haunt me, in a massive way. But it's true, I tell you. If you are a writer yourself, and you give the slightest toss about your work, then you know it's true.]

I wrote: 'I can't think of a nicer place to sit this spring over a glass of rosé and watch the boys and girls in the street outside smiling gaily to each other, and wondering where to go for a nosh.'

It appeared as: 'I can't think of a nicer place to sit this spring over a glass of rosé and watch the boys and girls in the street outside smiling gaily to each other, and wondering where to go for nosh.'

There is no length issue. This is someone thinking 'I'll just remove this indefinite article because Coren is an illiterate cunt and i know best'.

Well, you fucking don't.

This was shit, shit sub-editing for three reasons.

1) 'Nosh', as I'm sure you fluent Yiddish speakers know, is a noun formed from a bastardisation of the German 'naschen'. [Classic furious fake intellectualism coming up now, but it's pretty damn convincing.] It is a verb, and can be construed into two distinct nouns. One, 'nosh', means simply 'food'. You have decided that this is what i meant and removed the 'a'. I am insulted enough that you think you have a better ear for English than me. But a better ear for Yiddish? I doubt it. Because the other noun, 'nosh' means 'a session of eating' - in this sense you might think of its dual valency as being similar to that of 'scoff'. you can go for a scoff. or you can buy some scoff. the sentence you left me with is shit, and is not what i meant. Why would you change a sentnece aso that it meant something i didn't mean? [Look how angry I was! Look at the standard of typing. Jesus, I clearly didn't even glance over it once before I sent it.] I don't know, but you risk doing it every time you change something. And the way you avoid this kind of fuck up is by not changing a word of my copy without asking me, okay? it's easy. Not. A. Word. Ever.

2) I will now explain why your error is even more shit than it looks. You see, i was making a joke. I do that sometimes. I have set up the street as 'sexually-charged'. I have described the shenanigans across the road at G.A.Y.. I have used the word 'gaily' as a gentle nudge. And 'looking for a nosh' has a secondary meaning of looking for a blowjob. Not specifically gay, for this is soho, and there are plenty of girls there who take money for noshing boys. 'looking for nosh' does not have that ambiguity. the joke is gone. I only wrote that sodding paragraph to make that joke. And you've fucking stripped it out like a pissed Irish plasterer restoring a renaissance fresco and thinking jesus looks

4

shit with a bear so plastering over it. You might as well have removed the whole paragraph. I mean, fucking christ, don't you read the copy? [The mystery of this sentence – which baffled and entranced thousands of people – can be resolved when you learn that, in my furious key-hammering I accidentally failed to type the 'd' on the end of 'beard'. It was Jesus's beard I was imagining the plasterer leaving off. Though a number of correspondents later assumed I was referring to a little known Italian Renaissance tradition of picturing the Son of Man in close proximity to a bear, much as St Peter, say, is often seen with a lion.]

3) And worst of all. Dumbest, deafest, shittest of all, you have removed the unstressed 'a' so that the stress that should have fallen on 'nosh' is lost, and my piece ends on an unstressed syllable. When you're winding up a piece of prose, metre is crucial. Can't you hear? Can't you hear that it is wrong? It's not fucking rocket science. It's fucking pre-GCSE scansion. I have written 350 restaurant reviews for The Times and i have never ended on an unstressed syllable. Fuck. fuck, fuck, fuck.

I am sorry if this looks petty (last time i mailed a Times sub about the change of a single word i got in all sorts of trouble) but i care deeply about my work and i [all these uncapitalised 'i's, by the way, testify to the fact that I typed straight into an email – and I have grown so used to Word's automatic capitalising of that pronoun that I have lost the habit of doing it myself] hate to have it fucked up by shit subbing. I have been away, you've been subbing joe and hugo and maybe they just file and fuck off and think 'hey ho, it's tomorrow's fish and chips' - well, not me. I will not sleep now for several days. Possible more. weird, maybe. but that's how it is.

It strips me of all confidence in writing for the magazine [note the implied threat of resignation without ever coming close to actually doing it – for even in the froth of monstrous ire I know who pays the bills]. No exaggeration. i've got a review to write this morning and i really don't feel like doing it, for fear that some nuance is going to be removed from the final line, the pay-off, and i'm going to have another weekend ruined for me.

I've been writing for The Times for 15 years and i have never asked this before - i have never asked it of anyone i have written for - but I must insist, from now on, that i am sent a proof of every review i do, in pdf format, so i can check it for fuck-ups. and i must be sent it in good time in case changes are needed. It is the only way i can carry on in the job.

And, just out of interest, I'd like whoever made that change to email me and tell me why. Tell me the exact reasoning which led you to remove that word from my copy. [Nobody ever did.]

Right,

Sorry to go on. Anger, real steaming fucking anger can make a man verbose [note the anger starting to wear off already].

All the best [see what a reasonable, no-grudges-held sort of fellow I am],

Giles

And then I hit 'send', and went back downstairs, where my sausages were still steaming on the plate and my coffee was not yet cold.

By Monday morning my phone was ringing off the hook with *Times* people wanting to get to the bottom of things.

Bottom of what?

'This scandalous email.'

What scandalous email?

'The one you sent to Owen and Amanda and Ben.'

Have they complained?

'No.'

Then how come you've seen it?

'Everyone's seen it!'

Wretched Internet. By Tuesday, websites were full of what a terrible, terrible bastard I was, which made me awfully sad. Because it was only a rocket to fellow professionals who had done their job poorly and in the normal course of events it would never have got out into the world, nor would anyone have cared.

But media blogs and all sorts of forums for nameless losers whose inarticulate bitterness and lunacy would, in a pre-Internet world, have found no outlet, were suddenly saying I was a violent rapist, child murderer and bully for attacking my underlings like that. But they were not my underlings, they were just colleagues. I have no rank on *The Times* at all. I am not above anybody.

They were saying that it just goes to show what happens when someone goes on television and gets all up himself and arrogant. But it had nothing to do with being on telly. I've always been like that. Just look at my school reports.

The thing went 'viral'. People in offices with nothing to do and lonely onanists leaning back in their armchairs between YouPorn sessions, waiting for their juices to replenish, dug up my humble tirade and passed it on, and on and on.

Soon there were comedians singing songs about me on YouTube and then a film scene from Hitler's bunker was posted, in which the subtitles had been changed to make his loss of temper appear to be with the sub-editors who had bollixed my copy. And that was fair enough. I am sure, had he been around to see it, that the Führer would have been as enraged as I was.

On the plus side, my inbox was soon jamming with messages of support, hundreds of them. Mostly from fellow writers, including some top heroes of mine – Michael Atherton, Stephen Fry, David Baddiel – all of them hinting that my email expressed what they had always thought but had never dared to express – the awfulness of subs, the horror of what they do to our copy, and our impotence when it comes to doing anything about it.

How could great men like Athers and Fry not 'dare' to express their anger? What's so wrong with letting off a bit of steam?

Plenty, according to *The Guardian*, which by the end of the week had me on the front page – the front page! – with a photo of me looking all angry (but pretty damn saturnine and cool) and the headline 'Is this the maddest email ever?'

They actually saw my mild little reproach to a wayward colleague as evidence of mental illness. And by flagging the two-page piece on the front page they clearly thought it was going to help them sell newspapers. I was flattered. My own paper, *The Times*, never puts me on the front page. I was desperately hoping our editor would see it, and see what a big deal I was.

Inside, *The Guardian*, our great liberal upholder of free speech, old-fashioned news-gathering values, non-sensational, even-handed and, let's face it, really rather dreary journalism, had reprinted my email *in full*.

And not only that. It had dug out a previous email to *The Times* subs as well, the one rather naively hinted at in the more recent one. It was years old, sent way back in August 2002 – although *The Guardian* was using it as more evidence of my current insanity – and so I got a first chance to read it over again. It went as follows.

The quick brown fox jumps over the lazy dog. how fucking difficult is that? it's the sentence that bestrides the fucking book i reviewed for you. it is the sentence i wrote first in my fucking review. it is 35 fucking letters long, which is why i wrote that it was. and so some useless cunt subeditor decides to change it to 'jumps over A lazy dog' can you fucking count? can you see that that makes it a 33 letter sentence? so it looks as if i can't count, and the cunting author of the book, poor mr dunn, cannot count. the whole bastard book turns on the sentence being as i fucking wrote it. and that it is exactly 35 letters long. why do you meddle. what do you think you achieve with that kind of dumb-witted smart-arsery? why do you change things you do not understand without consulting. why do you believe you know best when you know fuck all. jack shit.

that is as bad as editing can be. fuck, i hope you're proud. it will be small relief for the author that nobody reads your poxy magazine.never ever ask me to write something for you. and don't pay me. i'd rather take £400 quid for assassinating a crack whore's only child in a revenge killing for a busted drug deal - my integrity would be less compromised.

jesus fucking wept i don't know what else to say.

Blimey, now that was a corker. Much better, much more succinct than the new one. I was delighted that it was finally seeing the light of day. And then – what was this? – they had found yet another, this time not sent to my subs at *The Times* but to the restaurant critic of the (now defunct – heh, heh, heh) *londonpaper*.

feargus,

I'm emailing to say that your review of osteria emilia, in most ways perfectly fine and good and spot on, pissed me off. i booked, as ever, under a pseudonym, that over made up italian bird did not have a fucking clue who i was (or even who baddiel was, who i ate with because he lives, like me, round the corner). Nor were there any kitchen staff peeking out of any porthole. i appreciate that you have to keep your column as lively as possible - and name dropping david i guess might be exciting for your readers (i'll certainly be doing it in my column) - but in your froth to show how folksy and incognito you are, you did your readers and the restaurant an immense disservice: you suggested that i got some special dispensation in eating a la carte. But if you'd spent a bit more time looking at your lunch menu, and a bit less gawping at me, you'd have noticed that it said, 'dishes from the evening a la carte menu are available at lunchtime, with some exceptions'.

You said 'i didn't have the brass neck to demand anything off the unavailable a la carte'. it makes you sound like an utter tit. you are not only a chippy fuck but a lazy journalist. 'brass neck'. learn to write, and take your head out of your arse, you fucking twat.

all the best

giles coren

Perfectly sound and normal for the most part, that one, becoming almost boring . . . and then POW! The foul-mouthed denouement comes in at the last to save the day. I was particularly fond of that one.

In total, *The Guardian* had published 2,000 words of mine without it costing them a penny. Now, I know that, with the exception of three or four very brilliant columnists, *The Guardian* is famously short on laughs, and that funny writers do not come cheap, but it still seemed, if not a monstrous liberty, then certainly a misdirecting of revenue streams.

Surely, I thought, it should be I, and not this *bien-pensant* bumrag of a paper, who gathers together all my apparently fascinating rage and madness and makes a literary point of it, and adds a sultry photo and charges an entry fee.

But 2,000 words wasn't really going to be enough for a whole book. If only I had written more emails like that. I could just bundle them up and – presto!

But I haven't. Well, actually I have. Loads. To building firms and garages and restaurants and shops and airlines and rail companies and taxi firms and schools and parking departments and police stations and pubs and dry cleaners and . . . they have all had their fall-outs and upshots and, one way or another, results. But I haven't kept them. I never thought of them as literary artefacts. Anger is a transitory thing: it wells up, it explodes, and then it is gone. And thank God for that. The last thing I wanted was to keep its evidence hanging around.

A number of publishers got in touch, suggesting that I should compile a book of pretend emails to people, written 'as if' I were really angry.

But anger is one thing – maybe the only thing – that cannot be faked. It is easy to tell someone you love them when you don't mean it. But it's practically impossible to tell them you hate them with any conviction, if you really don't.

And then I thought I could have a look back at some of the

stuff I've written before, and see if there was anything angry there. I doubted there would be. Because I just never thought of myself as an angry person.

Wrong. Practically every column is a gut-slobbering yodel of rage and bile at some – on reflection – perfectly inoffensive person, animal, inanimate object, fashion, law, plant . . .

And what is it with Nazis, fat people and *The Guardian*? I'm on about them all the time. I never give them a moment off, even though they have practically nothing to do with my life, and are extremely popular with some people, I'm sure. Why does my unconscious bleed such anger about them? Was I raped as a child by a fat Gestapo officer wearing socks and sandals?

What was (is) wrong with me? Are other people this angry? Are you? Is it healthy? Is it better out than in? I've heard that suppressing it gives you cancer. Or am I thinking of barbecued meat? Should I calm down? Should I take pills? Or just deep breaths? Should I really be in therapy? Or in a straitjacket?

I honestly don't know. But just in case you've ever been told by an angry wife or husband (your own or somebody else's) or girlfriend or boyfriend, parent, sibling, social worker, casualty nurse, traffic cop, best pal or parole officer, after a bit of a tiff, that 'what you need is anger management', well, here it is.

Travel

I was at a dismal press party the other day at some club in Whitehall, everyone wearing black tie, drunk on a distant tycoon's bar tab and weeping that they'd pissed their lives away (which they all had), when the former editor of a newspaper I once worked for accosted me and said, 'I've been reading a lot of your stuff lately, Giles. You're so down on everything, so quick to judge . . .' And then, before I could say 'No, I'm not, you drunk old fool,' he added, 'You should have taken the Tokyo job when we offered it to you. Travel broadens the mind.'

Yeah, sure it does. Have you ever met a foreign correspondent? They are, without exception, melodramatic, self-important, divorced, lonely and riddled with self-doubt. Their conversation is entirely anecdotal and largely fabricated and only has three subjects: drinking, fucking and dead friends. It's like world travel has turned them all into Irishmen. Foreign locations do not make a boring story or a boring man more interesting.

And yet there was a point in my late twenties when every editor I knew was trying to send me away to report from some foreign dog hole – Beijing, Delhi, Paris, New York, Berlin – because they thought it would make me a more rounded person. They wanted me to leave my comfy home in north London and my cushy job at the cutting edge of make-it-all-up-and-put-some-jokes-in journalism to go to a bloody war zone, because it would 'broaden my mind'.

Why would I want to broaden my mind? I like it narrow. It's easier to find my way around it. You don't get lost and you get where you want to without too much wear on the brakes and steering.

'But Giles,' these editors would point out, 'it's such a waste when you speak all those foreign languages.' And it's true, I do speak two or three. But only so I can tell foreigners I meet in Britain to fuck off home in a language they can understand.

All my life people have been trying to make me travel. When I was 16 my school tried to send me to America on exchange for a term to help me 'grow up'. I refused to go, reasoning that there was no way hanging out in some doofus-y Californian college and losing my virginity to a nut-brained blonde tart who only fancied me because of my accent, and getting stoned every night on the beach and learning to surf was going to help me grow up. So I did another term at school as usual. That showed them.

When I was 17, my German class went on a month-long exchange to a grammar school in the suburbs of Munich, where we were supposed to learn what modern Germany was really like away from all the clichés. What I learned was that all Germans are huge, blond Nazis who wear lederhosen and eat garlic sausage for breakfast. And the girls have hairy armpits. And there's no need to learn their stupid language because they all speak fluent English by the middle of their teens because they are still hell-bent on world domination.

In my early twenties I worked in a shop in Paris for a year and discovered that the French are petty, racist, sex-obsessed and lazy. The most narrow-minded people in the world. How could they possibly have made me broader?

I have travelled all over the world and have learned only that I hate people who travel most of all. With their cameras and their bum bags and their maps and their smattering of the lingo and their cultural sensitivity, and their rough guides and even rougher girlfriends.

You go to their houses. They have carpets on the wall. Carpets on the wall, I tell you. Because they have bought so many bloody carpets that there is no more room for them on the floor any more. All over Turkey, Persia and Afghanistan they have been unable to say no to those scary little moustached crooks in curly-toed slippers who drag you into their stinking hovels to drink filthy tea and look at their manky carpets ('I give you a special deal, my friend. My name is Abdul, I am student, I like very much Mrs Tetcher').

I tell you, if some Turk wants £500 off me I would rather he whacked me on the head with his hubbly bubbly down a dark street and stole it out of my pocket. At least then I wouldn't have to schlep some foetid rug all the way to the airport and go and salvage it from the extra-large luggage counter at Heathrow with all the snowboarders and cellists and Dutch school-teachers on cycle tours.

And what is a broad mind anyway? It is a general tendency to accept things. When your 15-year-old daughter tells you she's pregnant but she isn't sure who the father is unless it's that bloke she's been visiting in prison, and you respond by asking whether she's hoping for a boy or a girl, you are said to be broad-minded. Is that a good thing? And did you get like this because you spent your gap year in Goa? Or is it because you were dropped on your head as a baby?

You don't travel because it broadens the mind. You travel because it's sunny, the drugs are cheaper, prostitution is legal, there's no speed limit and there's an England match on the Saturday.

Travel broadens nothing but the spectrum of exotic venereal diseases to which you are potentially exposed, the extent of your homesickness, your experience of pre-industrial medical standards, the sculpture of exotic fag packets you have been building since you were 14 and the collection of foreign banknotes you have under the glass top on the table in the spare bedroom.

Fat People

I have every sympathy with David Walker, the Lanarkshire GP who proposed a tax on chocolate as a way to ease the obesity crisis and reduce the spread of type 2 diabetes, only to see it narrowly voted down at the annual conference of the British Medical Association.

Like Dr Walker, I was appalled to learn that fatties across the nation are consuming their full daily recommended intake of calories in the form of sweeties alone, over and above the mounds of cack they swill down at the times of day the rest of us call 'meal times', but which for an increasing proportion of Britons merely represent thrice-daily upward spikes in the ceaseless, rolling gobble that constitutes their lives.

Like him, I am horrified by how much it costs the NHS to look after so many people who have made themselves ill simply through a lack of willpower and/or self-respect. It's not just type 2 that is in danger of crippling the health service. It is joint replacements, gastric banding, heart disease, other organ failures and all the respiratory problems that follow in obesity's gigantic, swaggering wake. The total annual cost of human fatness to the NHS is estimated at £1 billion a year. One billion pounds! That's an awful lot of Toblerones.

Then there's the cost to the economy in sick pay and incapacity benefits arising from obesity: a staggering £2.5 billion per year. And, of course, the extra transport costs linked to obesity – which run to £250 million annually – because the fatter we grow, the fewer people can fit in a bus or train, and the more fuel is required to move each human.

So it comes to something like £4 billion a year that fat people are costing our economy, not to mention the immense personal harm they are doing to themselves. Over the past ten years Britons have, on average, put on six pounds each. Two thirds of us are overweight (that's you, fatty!), 10 per cent of premature deaths in this country are fatness-related and by next year obesity will take over from smoking as Britain's biggest preventable killer. And it has got to the point where I, like Dr Walker, have lost faith in humanity's ability to save itself.

Like Dr Walker I believe that the answer lies in taxation. You have to hit people where it hurts most, which in the case of fat people is in their wallets, because literally hitting them (fun though it is) doesn't hurt them at all, what with their being so fat.

But where I differ from Dr Walker is that I do not believe in taxing chocolate. First of all, the money thus raised will not get anywhere near to recouping the £4 billion a year we are owed by the gut-buckets; and second, it would constitute an infringement of the rights of normally sized people to eat chocolate.

Personally, I love a few squares of posh chocolate with a cup of tea. I'll guzzle a Snickers with the best of them if I've exhausted myself playing football, or simply chasing fat people across Hampstead Heath with a stick. But why should I – with my healthy weight of twelve and a half stone, respectable body mass index (BMI) of 24 and damn near supernatural total body fat percentage of 12.5 – have to pay more for it?

And if the choccy tax were extended to high-fat fast foods, as has been mooted, that again would penalise me. Sometimes I need a Big Mac to keep me going, or an entire KFC bargain bucket. But they can't hurt me because I'm not fat. And never will be.

Calories are not like cigarettes, alcohol and guns – they are not, in themselves, bad for you. To tax them is to punish us all for the sins of the porkers, to keep the whole class in after school because Fatty couldn't control himself.

Taxing the things that contain the calories is cumbersome, unworkable and fiscally inadequate. What we have to do is tax fat people directly. I admit that this is a form of head tax (or rather, in this case, an arse tax) of the kind that has led to all sorts of social unrest in the past, but don't worry: fat people are far too lazy to riot.

The key here is to make people pay more income tax the fatter they are, so as to incentivise weight loss and repair the damage done to the economy. And the obvious way to create a tax that is both income- and blubber-related is to take each individual's annual tax liability (as derived by the current system) and then multiply it by the square root of his BMI over a hundred. So, where L is the normal tax liability:

$$X = L\left(\frac{\sqrt{BMI}}{100}\right)$$

This way, for example, if your BMI is 36, which is halfway between obese and morbidly obese, you would pay 6 per cent more tax than a normal person. If you currently pay £5,000, you will pay £5,300. It's not a lot in punitive terms but it will comfortably raise the sums we need, and it will give fat people an opportunity to choose between paying up or laying off the sweeties – which is only fair in a sophisticated democracy such as ours.

Had Dr Walker taken this far more evolved and fairer taxation plan to the BMA, I am sure that they would have approved it to a man.

IN OTHER NEWS: *to help tackle obesity in children, the government has announced a plan to weigh children in schools and inform parents of the results. However, schools will not be allowed to use the medical term 'obese' in their reports, because it might cause offence. So I suppose concerned parents will just have to read between the lines when it comes to deciphering such cryptically encoded messages as, for example, these:*

'Dear Mr and Mrs Wisbeech, your son, Arnold, has been weighed in the balance . . . and broke it.'

'Dear Mr and Mrs Funt, your daughter, Ellie, has not been weighed today as planned, because when she took off her dress prior to mounting the scales the doctor laughed so hard he had an embolism.'

'Dear Mr Jarse, your son, Hugh, was weighed today. We are not saying he is fat, we are just saying that from next term we will be charging fees for both of him.'

'Dear Mrs Hunt, your son, Eric, was weighed today and the school doctor will be writing to you with the results just as soon as he can break free of Eric's gravitational pull.'

'Dear Mrs Hunt, your other son, Warwick, was also weighed. Tell you what, if you can guess his weight to the nearest stone, we'll forget about all those broken chairs.'

Queues

They've introduced a £3 queue-barging licence at Luton airport, and it's the best idea I have heard in ages. It has existed for some time at such provincial airports as Leeds Bradford, Bristol and Liverpool, and is nothing more complicated than an extra little fee you can pay on top of your ticket, which means that, when you are dashing for your plane and get to that soul-destroyingly lengthy queue at security, you can barge straight to the front with impunity. Now it is to be rolled out, with a bit of luck, nationwide.

'Oi, mate, can't you see there's an effing queue?' the tracksuited plebs will cry. And you will reply: 'Yes, my good people, I can indeed see that there is a queue – but can YOU see this official get-out-of-queue-free card which I presciently purchased some days ago in anticipation of just such an eventuality as this?'

And through you will blithely march, perhaps pausing briefly to doff your fedora, so as to rile the oiks just that little bit more.

Oh, what a marvellous start to a holiday that would be. I am going to buy one of these queue passes now, this second, and go to Luton this afternoon, and barge into a few queues just for the fun of it – even though I'm not flying anywhere.

I think the principle should be extended to queues everywhere, not just airports. I want to buy a Queue-Bargers' Gold Card that will allow me to barge queues in the supermarket, at the post office and in the bank. I want to hoick old ladies out of the way at cash machines – interminably ferreting in their weeny purses, failing to grasp the simplest rudiments of electronic screen interfacing, and all to withdraw a single moth-eaten fiver

– and, when they protest, simply wave my ticket at them and say: 'Tough titties, Grandma, Giley's got a waiver.'

I want to trundle my luggage to the front of the unfeasibly long taxi queue at Paddington station and wave my barger's indemnity licence at furious Belgian businessmen who cannot believe that such a thing exists, and curse themselves for not bringing their fold-up bicycle.

I want to sail to the front of queues at the cinema and at Lord's and Wembley, and as the uniformed security men move towards me simply flash my card.

'Queue-Bargers' Express?' they will say. 'That'll do nicely.'

And why stop at queue-barging? There are all sorts of antisocial or illegal activities for which I could do with a licence. I'll happily pay a few quid a week for a card that lets me smoke in restricted areas, buy booze at four in the morning, ignore speed limits, sleep with other men's wives, fart loudly in restaurants without people making huffy remarks, and clip teenagers round the ear for walking three abreast down the pavement, saying 'like' all the time and being generally shabby and annoying.

As dozens of former schoolmasters and employers have observed, I have tended to go through life assuming that there is one set of rules for me, and one for everybody else. And it may yet turn out to be true.

The Boat Race

I'm going to a Boat Race party tomorrow: lovely afternoon in Putney, barbecue in the garden with a bit of luck, a jug of Pimm's, and then down to the river to watch the dark and light blues battle it out in the oldest tussle on the water, cheering like billyo for . . . wait, remind me for a second just exactly why in the world I am supposed to give a rat's arse who wins?

The Boat Race is the most incomprehensible of all sporting events. Why on earth do tens of thousands of ordinary Londoners gather every year along the banks of our most famous river to watch 16 gigantic morons attempting to assert by raw muscle the primacy of one or other ancient, irrelevant university?

How can it be, when everybody is so down on Oxford and Cambridge, so unfeasibly narked by their refusal to fill their colleges with knuckle-dragging working-class thickos in the name of equality, that hundreds of thousands of people who didn't attend either take sides each year in their preposterous tug-o'-war on water?

Rowing! It's not even a sport. It's just a measuring system for brute force, ambition and the ability to subjugate oneself to a collective will. It's Nazism with paddles. It's a keep-fit pastime for pituitary cases who are too dim for rugby.

I can understand why it used to be thought exciting, back in the days when Oxbridge graduates ran the world. The masses no doubt felt that they had to come down on one side or another, as a light blue or a dark, and shout their yokel throats hoarse in the hope of passing for a damned good man.

And I guess that back then, when Oxbridge graduates were

not ashamed of the elitism of their education, they continued to care how well their alma mater did long after they had left it behind. My father, for example, was a fiend for the thing, a dark blue all his life. But he was proud of having gone to Oxford and a bit of his heart was always there, stranded in a small, wet town off the M40.

I, on the other hand, care less about the Boat Race than the national kabaddi championships of Bangladesh. And I was a Blue, for heaven's sake (well, OK, a half-Blue for Eton fives). I can get quite partisan about *University Challenge*, but that's because knowledge is a relevant thing to measure in the context of universities, and I do enjoy the annual proof that Oxford and Cambridge kids are just marginally less dim than kids everywhere else.

But the Boat Race is not even contested by students, really. Not in the real sense of the word. It's just a load of huge Canadian dorks filling in time between Olympics doing land economy diplomas at an imaginary college being coxed by the lone undergraduate in the boat – some random undernourished midget who doesn't mind getting up at 5 a.m. every day because he doesn't have any mates, and builds his entire social persona around the joke that he enjoys coxing because he gets to boss tall people around.

Still, I'll watch it, like I do every year, in the vague hope that they'll interview some pretty girls and one of the boats will sink. Or, better still, both of them.

Parcelforce

One bright, dusty, midsummer-quiet afternoon last week the doorbell rang and I looked out of the window (to avoid making the long descent from study to street only to find a kid with a box of J-Cloths for sale or some pair of credulous bozos with good news about the Lord) and saw that it was the postman.

Well, not exactly the postman. What I had seen was a Parcelforce van, which is better still. Now that Parcelforce is the large-object wing of the Post Office, the Parcelforce guy is more exciting than Postie himself, since Postie is now protected by safety-in-the-workplace guidelines from carrying anything that I might eat, drink, read or hang on the wall.

So I bustled to the door full of the joy of the day, ready to hail the fellow with my breeziest 'good afternoon' and take delivery of whatever jolliness he had in his bag. But as I opened it, my hair and whiskers were fair blown back by loud music, a thumping beat and the shouted words: 'I'm gonna **** you, bitch! Yeah, bitch! Yeah bitch! I'm gonna **** you, bitch! Yeah, bitch! Yeah, bitch!'

I was more than a little startled. The postman in question, however – a wiry, sullen-looking fellow, maybe 25 years old, with a Parcelforce beanie pulled low on his brow – seemed blissfully unbothered as he wordlessly handed me an electronic thing to sign. And indeed, when I looked out past him towards the noise, I saw that it emanated from his own vehicle, the aforementioned little red van, as little and red as Postman Pat's, which was double-parked outside my house, in my quiet suburban street, with the windows open and this loud, aggressive rap booming from it: 'I'm gonna **** you, bitch! Yeah, bitch! Yeah bitch!'

As he held the electronic thing in my face, the postman (and I insist on calling him a postman, despite his no doubt being officially known at Parcelforce as a 'delivery solutions operative', or some such, because he was delivering my post and was in the pay of Royal Mail Group Ltd) was actually nodding his head to this vile music.

When I was a kid, our postman, Derek, used to whistle as he came down the path with our letters. He may have been whistling a tune whose original words were, 'I'm gonna **** you, bitch!' but I doubt it. It was usually 'Colonel Bogey'.

I honestly didn't know where to look. My house is 50 yards from a primary school. I might have been a little old lady (more than likely if you're looking for a front door to be answered at three in the afternoon) or a mother with children. How can it possibly be acceptable for a man from the Royal Mail, the Royal bloody Mail, going about what is in theory Her Majesty's business, to be declaring as he rings your mother's doorbell, my mother's doorbell, anybody's mother's doorbell, on a quiet June afternoon: 'I'm gonna **** you, bitch! Yeah, bitch! Yeah bitch!'?

The man can listen to that kind of sick, sexist drivel in his own time, if he wants. And I dare say that the manager of whatever rap band it was he was listening to will have some excuse up his sleeve about how the song only reflects the sexist and aggressive mores of the street, without specifically endorsing them, but, I swear, if he showed up round my place with that kind of specious bilge I would specifically endorse his face for him.

I grasp that people under 25, people born into the iPod age, cannot conceive of music as anything but a constant backdrop. Music is no longer a thing to be enjoyed for its own sake, at gigs and festivals and in pubs and clubs and at home on a stereo, but is a vain and impotent declaration of self to be blared from cars and phones and laptops and headsets at all times – a constant somatic comfort to the dull, blunt, flabby modern brain. But to crawl the streets of the city playing offensive rap music on full volume with the windows wound down is the sort of carry-on you expect from teenage hoodlums, stabby little respec'-seekers and bug-eyed gang-rapists on crack. Not an employee of the Royal Mail. Not your bloody postman.

I didn't know what to say to the man. So I didn't say anything. Maybe if I had he would have shanked me for dissing his tunes. I don't know, maybe that's what they teach postmen to do these days.

Maybe, with all these threats to its business from email and private sector courier companies, the Post Office is planning to go a different way to modernise. Maybe it is going to train postmen to carry blades, slouch down the street with their trousers round their knees, pouting and scowling and playing rape anthems on their phones, and asking people what they are staring at, so that they can stab them to death.

Or, I don't know, maybe, 'I'm gonna **** you, bitch! Yeah bitch! Yeah bitch!' is the message the Royal Mail is really trying to send us.

The tune, and its bone-headed, soul-sickening lyrics, stayed with me all day. Try how I might, I simply could not dislodge it from my brain, even with a constant, quiet, wistful repetition of 'Postman Pat, Postman Pat, Postman Pat and his black and white cat . . .'

Curry

A survey of fast-food preferences by Mintel (always there with the really important stuff in a time of global crisis) has revealed that for the first time Chinese food has overtaken Indian as Britain's favourite takeaway.

I am amazed that it took this long. Chinese is sooooo much nicer than Indian. I mean, who in the world eats Indian deliberately? Round my way the good Chinese closes at 10, the Thai at 11, and the myriad Indians then stay open till midnight and beyond. So it's only a very badly planned evening that ends with four tin boxes of miscellaneous brown slop, gritty rice randomly scattered with scary pink and yellow grains, and a paper bag of giant crisps, partially smashed.

I think that must be how Indian food established its fabled supremacy in this country (chicken tikka masala being Britain's national dish and all that): simply by being the only thing left available when fat, poorly educated men stagger out of the pub.

Taking the lids off in the kitchen and carrying the metal trays of wobbling curry through into the telly room, one is always reminded of those models they used to explain why the *Herald of Free Enterprise* went down when the car deck flooded.

Except the *Herald of Free Enterprise* didn't fill with always-mysteriously-goaty brown gravy, full of fleshy flotsam that makes your mouth feel next morning like you spent the night giving mouth-to-mouth to an entire stag party.

Chinese, on the other hand, is always yummy: lovely plump pink things frazzed in hot oil with a spritz of garlic and chilli, steaming dumplings, brightly coloured nibbly bits and, crucially, delicious piles of vegetables – choi sum, bok choi or gai lan – stir-fried with a splash of something rich and dark to give it a bit of body.

Ask if they have 'anything green' in an Indian restaurant and the waiter will glance shiftily at the kitchen door then lean down and whisper: 'Well, the mutton's been on the turn since Tuesday . . .'

Polly Toynbee

I don't know if you've had a chance yet to read a book by Polly Toynbee and David Walker called *Unjust Rewards* – personally I've seen only extracts in the paper – in which the two *Guardian* stalwarts interview loads of rich people and discover that . . . they're not very nice.

Who would have thought? It's lucky we have *The Guardian* to get to the nub of things for us with its unique blend of snobbery, bitterness, jealousy and thwarted ambition, cobbled together with the tawdry and risible clichés its readers have thrilled to for years.

Dave and Polly begin with a trip to the 20th floor of Canary Wharf, only to find it 'marbled'. Is it really, Dave? Is it, Polly? Or do you just need to write 'marbled' to ram home your clunky, 1970s them-and-us dichotomy? Because two sentences later the same exact spot is suddenly 'a gilded new town in the sky'. Ooh, gilded and marbled. How rich these people must be.

Polly and Dave chat for a while to some bankers and lawyers (hawk, spit) and discover that the fiends 'utterly misjudged the magnitude of their privilege' and 'put themselves inside a golden enclave'. Marbled, gilded, and golden. Dave and Polly are good. They should do bathrooms.

'They could scarcely deny they had money,' write Dave and Polly, as if any decent human being would. And then they tell us that they, Dave and Polly, are not so much angry as disappointed: 'What we had hoped for was more awareness, some recognition that their position needed explaining and even justification.' You really hoped for that, Polly? Really, Dave? Then you're even stupider than you come across on paper.

And they get stupider. And more bitter. And more teacherly and smug. 'As a group [the rich people] were less intelligent,' they crow, 'less intellectually inquisitive, less knowledgeable and, despite their good schools, less broadly educated than high-flyers in other professions.'

But we knew that. City lawyers and bankers have always been thick. They work inhuman hours at pointless jobs for their capitalist slave-masters and die young without really knowing their wives, their children or themselves. It's a horrible life. And they are given a lot of money to make up for it.

What are you telling us, Polly? That they'd be happier living naked on a heath and eating dormice? We know that. They know that. Nobody cares. Shut up.

And then Dave and Polly write: 'Their high salaries were not a sign of any obvious superiority.' Well, hell, guys, did you expect them to be? You're meant to be socialists. You really went grovelling in there, tugging your forelocks and expecting these people, on the basis of their wealth, to be in some way good or interesting? How stupid can you be? Your ideas are so thin and your politics so hackneyed and hamstrung by prejudice that you actually made me sympathise with the very rich. And I never thought anyone would be able to do that.

The next day, in my favourite paper's always-gripping education section ('Down wiv' Eton!'), there was another extract from the book, in which Dave and Polly had joined some state school kids from Brent on a trip to Oxford (I bet the kids were delighted).

The clichés here were more delicious still. Not only did the word 'spires' appear twice in the same short extract, but the lawns, bless them, were 'manicured'. Except they're not, Polly. They're just mown. Same as everywhere else. You don't have to be rich, or posh, or evil to mow the bloody lawn. They mow the lawn on council estates too. It's you, Polly, and you, Dave, who are trying to present Britain as a cartoonish, divided society to suit your own arrogant, dim-witted, outdated *Weltanschauung*.

Dave and Polly take the kids to St John's, which (no coincidence, I'm sure) is Oxford's richest college by some way: 'Here was a room of their own, with their own bathroom, use of a kitchen . . .'

Their own bathroom? I very much doubt it, even at St John's. Certainly not at Keble, next door to St John's, where I was a student. Six or eight to a bathroom at best (not all at the same time, alas). Get some perspective.

Despite Dave and Polly's best doom-mongering efforts, the kids on the trip show great enthusiasm for going to Oxford. So Dave and Polly leap in: 'Did the Brent students know that over half the students at Oxford and Cambridge come from private schools? They had no idea and it shocked them.'

Yeah, that's right, Polly, you step in and piss on their dreams, why don't you. Tell them they've got no chance. It's your way, after all. (Furthermore, that statistic was another gross exaggeration, as a correction in *The Guardian* admitted the following day.)

It's not Oxford itself that holds back kids like this, it's sour old Trots like Toynbee.

Polly and Dave go on to contrast, with toe-curling naivety, the 'kindly earnestness and bright whiteness' of the Oxford students with 'the mostly black Brent kids in urban fashions with sharply razored, sculpted and combed hairstyles', the prose dripping with that familiar and uniquely *Guardian* fetishising of black youth that seems to drip with middle-aged female lust for the noble savage. It's positively Victorian.

'Here on display,' wrote Dave and Polly, 'was the great fissure in class, race, style, attitude, background . . .' No, here were children. The fissure is in your minds. In your sad, tawdry imaginations. Part of a world you need to believe in to believe you have any value left as commentators.

'The Brent students will likely find themselves in a rust-stained concrete former polytechnic not far from home . . .' write Dave and Polly in tear-stained conclusion. More clichés, more fatalism.

But how dare she/he condemn them like that to their doom? And how dare she/he stigmatise former polytechnics in that way?

Rust-stained, for God's sake. How can these new universities hope to attract decent students, and be taken seriously in the academic world, if the rotten Stalinist dimwits of *The Guardian* opinion pages are so quick to dismiss them?

Dogs

The death of Jaden Joseph Mack, mauled to death by two domestic dogs in his grandmother's home near Caerphilly, caused a ripple of anxiety in some quarters, muted calls for stricter licensing of dangerous breeds, and that was about it. Move along now. Nothing to see here.

Nothing, except a human infant shredded to burger meat by domestic pets. My God, the fuss they made over Baby P. Over Maddie. Over Sarah Payne. Over James Bulger. When the boneheaded popular press can use a toddler's death to hammer such traditional bogeymen as paedophiles, social workers, 'evil' young boys and invisible foreign ne'er-do-wells, it goes at it with a drooling, wide-eyed, sociopathic bloodlust, calling for hangings, sackings and ridiculous legislative upheavals. But when it's done by a Staffordshire bull terrier, the very breed of dog most likely to have been tied up outside the shop while its owner goes in to buy a 'red top' tabloid, they have nothing to say.

And government is no better, to be honest. It is astonishing to think that when a fox is torn apart by dogs in a cold field on a foggy morning, Parliament devotes 700 hours of debate to stamping it out. But when a human child is torn apart by dogs in his or her nan's front room (it's always the grandmother – usually not much more than 30 herself), Parliament does nothing. Nothing.

Now, I'm never going to stop the right-wing media from wildly overreacting to child deaths as a way to excoriate the same old demons, but I can at least beg them, on my knees, to overreact for once to something I care about. And to call for dogs to be banned. All dogs. Now.

Anything less – outlawing breeds, renovating the licensing system, muzzling potential offenders – simply won't work. And the 1991 Dangerous Dogs Act is, I am afraid, bunkum. It is concerned primarily with a lot of mealy-mouthed exceptions and exemptions that make it impossible to prosecute owners unless they are caught on camera with a Japanese tosa, deliberately feeding it live toddlers in front of a policeman and six witnesses.

The act specifies breeds only ambiguously, and does not even cover Staffordshire bull terriers – the chosen legal street weapon of every pock-faced teenage stabber and crack-dealing hoody in the land – which were implicated not only in the killing of Jaden, but in the savaging of 22-month-old Kira Neal in Bournemouth on 3 August 2007, and of two-year-old Paige Allison in Blackburn on 27 April of the same year, and of two-year-old Joseph Johnson outside a fish and chip shop in Hull on 17 September 2008.

Not that a ban on 'Staffies' would have helped 13-month-old Archie-Lee Hirst, slaughtered by a Rottweiler at his grandparents' home in Chald Lane, Wakefield, the day after Boxing Day 2007.

They've got to go. Dogs have just got to go. All dogs. Just to be safe. I'm not saying a spaniel represents a mortal danger to toddlers (indeed, if you shoot a toddler yourself your spaniel will merely go over and point at it, and then your golden retriever will bring it back, and your Dalmatian will bury it and then forget where it left it), but the problem is that owners will always get round breed-specific laws by crossing their murderous animals with others, as a disguise.

Germany, where the import of Staffies is illegal, has shown us some of the way, and Israel has gone one better, making the breed illegal altogether – and I doubt there are many who flout that little law. You don't go breeding dogs to scare your neighbours when you know that one false snarl and a helicopter gunship's going to whoop into view, flatten your house, your nan's house and your local school, and then blame it on the dog.

And don't think for a minute that I would consider such a

response disproportionate. I hate dogs. I am currently in the process of moving house purely and simply because my beautiful, leafy Camden street is the most turd-bespaffed thoroughfare in England.

This is because I live down the road from a housing estate surveyed by CCTV cameras where the inhabitants know that if they let their little fighting dog uncurl a bronze they will be filmed and fined. So they come down the nice, middle-class streets purely to unload faeces. It seems almost a matter of honour.

These dogs get walked each day only for as long as it takes to smoke two Royals and gob a greeny at a tree. They don't even get as far as Hampstead Heath, only two minutes up the road (or perhaps they choose not to go there – the *bien-pensant* middle classes with their wellies and Labs having made of the Heath such a stinking dog toilet you'd be mad to cross it without an anthrax suit).

Every morning, on my three-minute stroll to buy a paper, I encounter at least three brand new turds, on my side of the street alone, glistening in the sun. When the snow was falling, and the street-cleaning guy couldn't get through, there were layers of turd interleaved with the layers of frozen snow like some terrible *millefeuille* of *merde*. And the thaw brought hourly uncoverings of newly revealed hound crap, kept fresh by the sub-zero temperatures, the goodness sealed in, the scent released gradually over the days.

Kill all the dogs. Kill all of them. I'll do it if you can't face it, and toss the rigid corpses on the fatty flames with a pitchfork.

For most of human history, dogs were needed. We bred them to do jobs we couldn't, or didn't want to do ourselves. And now we have machines. And don't bait bears. The keeping of dogs is a primitive throwback to a state of nature that was nasty, brutish and poo-smelling. It has no relevance now. We must grow out of dogs just as we grew out of horses (which was not, as many think, because we invented the car, but because we invented synthetic glue).

And please, don't come to me with dogs as companions for the lonely. Ye gods, has society sunk so low that we must leave it to stinking mutts to solace the old, the forgotten and the lost?

Some dogs may be innocent of killing. But all are guilty of crapping. When we were young, and one kid wouldn't own up to his crime, they put the whole class in detention, regardless of individual guilt. My plan is like that, only with dogs. Except then you kill them.

I have felt this for a long time but always kept quiet out of respect for my many dog-owning friends. But the story of Jaden's death was so awful, so grim and primal and nightmarish – like a modern Little Red Riding Hood where the gran survives at the expense of the child – that I cannot tolerate delay.

And yet it will never happen. And poor Jaden will be forgotten. His little face will never stare up at you from the newspaper rack, above a headline telling you that the campaign starts here, and that he didn't die in vain.

And that is because unlike paedos and lefty social workers, dogs, through their feckless, simpering owners, really do rule the world.

Vegetarianism

A recent report in the *Journal of the American Dietetic Association* appears to show that teenagers and young adults are more likely to suffer from eating disorders if they have tried being vegetarian.

And I'm, like, 'duh!' (I'm like that because that is how American teenagers talk, you understand, and I want them to understand what I am about to say). And the reason that I am, as I say, like, 'duh!' is that vegetarians are more likely to suffer from eating disorders because vegetarianism *is* an eating disorder.

It's a better eating disorder than many others, because at least it doesn't make you fat, and in general it doesn't cause you to wither away and die. But it does make you pale and flaky and unbelievably tedious to be around.

Vegetarianism is a cry for help. A sadly transparent attempt to exercise control over your body, which you feel the need to do for psychological reasons of which you are probably unaware. It's why so many vegetarians have tattoos and exotic piercings (you know it's true). It's why anarchists, squatters, G20 protesters and art students are usually vegetarians.

Frustrated that they cannot, and never will, control the world, or anything else of any significance, they starve themselves and carve holes in their bodies. It's as primitive a lifestyle as there is. It's why the very oldest religions eschew meat altogether, and others eschew some forms of it – because one exercises what control one can in the shadow of a mighty God with miserable little gestures of abstinence.

It's why vegetarians are mostly girls. Because vegetarianism is a way of controlling one's food intake without drawing attention to one's vanity.

'Don't mind me,' they say when they come to your house for lunch. 'I'll just have the vegetables.'

And you think: 'It's immaterial to me what you put in your mouth, darling, because I can tell from the state of you that you're going to be in my downstairs bog with your fingers down your throat in half an hour, spraying whatever you've pecked at all over the Armitage Shanks.'

It's the same with all these bogus wheat allergies and dairy intolerances – codswallop the lot of them. Just a way of not having to say: 'I'm on a diet so that I will look nicer and people will fancy me.' Vegetarians never love food. They merely tolerate it.

I wholeheartedly concur with the notion that we in the developed world eat too much meat. We absolutely do. Current meat consumption levels are unhealthy for the people and a drain on the planet's resources. The neo-Malthusian projection that says there is not enough land to feed the nine billion people who will be living here by 2020 unless most of the meat-producing land is turned over to vegetable crops (or something) is probably not too wide of the mark.

So the thing to do is to eat less meat, not none. You don't make meat a moral issue and campaign to end it. You just lay off it a bit. That way there will be plenty to go round, the land will be able to yield its bounty much more efficiently (after all, without cow crap to nourish the soil, how are your precious carrots going to grow all big and juicy?), nobody will have to die of heart disease and we'll all be able to scoff a juicy steak from time to time.

Meat is not something to be eradicated, like cancer. Its total destruction is not a moral imperative for the human race. Nor is meat something with absolutely no visible function whose continued existence is a baffling mystery, like wasps or men's nipples or television chefs. Meat tastes good. It carries vitamins and minerals with a unique efficiency that is critical to the maintenance of a healthy life. And it gives pigs, quite literally, a reason to live.

To eat no meat at all is to take an extreme position in an area where extremism is not called for. People always say 'Hitler was a vegetarian', as if that were some sort of paradox, some sort of surprise. Well it isn't to me. He was a vegetarian because he was an extremist. He was incapable of doing things by halves. Annoyed that the banking system in Weimar Germany was largely controlled by Jews (as it certainly was), he might well have proposed a programme to make banking more attractive to Gentiles, offered some economics scholarships to giant Bavarian pork-munchers, dragged some idle Christian dimbos out of the beer halls and taught them to count . . . but he didn't, he decided to kill every Jew in Europe.

In exactly the same way, had he been a more even-tempered man, he might well have reacted to the meat-heavy traditional German diet (which presumably didn't agree with him) by simply ladling more sauerkraut onto his plate and holding back on the wurst, by eating a bit of salad occasionally, and by not having ham for breakfast. But no. He was an extremist. He had to eat NO! MEAT! EVER! AGAIN!

The ideological road from nut cutlets to Belsen is straight, and short.

Skiing

When I was 18 years old my best friend, Jules Harrison, was killed in a skiing accident.

We had lunch at Pizza Hut in Hampstead the day before he left for Zermatt. He parked his father's Rover (the one we had crashed in Fitzjohn's Avenue, drunk, aged 16, a couple of years before) right outside. The restaurant is a Starbucks now (obviously), and you certainly aren't allowed to park outside.

I was disappointed that he was going. I had only two friends then, and could ill afford to lose one of them for even a week, let alone a lifetime.

'Skiing's for losers, man,' I told him, jealously. 'It's for poncey French tossers and Sloanes and malcos who can't play football.'

'It's only because you can't do it,' said Jules. 'And stop saying "man" all the time.'

It's true, I couldn't ski. I'd been on a school trip once, wearing borrowed ladies' salopettes and an awful woolly hat, and I'd floundered miserably on the nursery slopes with a group of Italian toddlers, terrified for my life, while a nut-brown Austrian instructor barked the kind of bone-chilling orders that an Englishman can take, from an Austrian, for only so long. And occasionally Jules, a famously skilled and fearless skier, would rocket across the group, backwards, on one ski, smoking a cigar and laughing.

I hated skiing. I hated the lack of control. I hated the sliding. I hated the stupid T-bar lift, which you fall off and then aren't allowed to get back on to but have to slide all the way down to the bottom on your arse (because you can't ski) and then queue again for it with a load of foreign bastards who can't even play cricket. And then fall off again.

I hated the huge uncomfortable boots that made blisters on your shins, and which you couldn't walk in at lunch time except heel-and-toeing like Robocop, clumpety, clumpety clump.

I hated the chairlifts going up, up, up above the bloody trees, and then sometimes the mountain falls away on the other side and it's 3,000ft down – woooaaaahhh – and you think you're going to throw up, and it suddenly stops in mid-air because some fat Swiss fool has dropped his Rolex. And you swing there. Silently. Rocking and squeaking in the breeze. Holding your breath . . . and then a fighter plane on manoeuvres, piloted by some reckless Italian soldier boy in Ray-Bans, swoops low and slices the cable, and you fall, helpless, to your death, still strapped into your steel chair.

Or you go over a cliff edge. Those crazy, mental corners. There's ice, your skis slide out and out, your pathetic learner's snowplough falls to bits and there's no option but to throw yourself to the floor to avoid hurtling over the edge. So you do, and you bang your head only gently. But still there is epidural haematoma, and you die.

'Walk-and-die' syndrome. Some holiday.

And if you don't die, you break things. The kids in school after the Christmas holidays with their legs in plaster, everybody signing the cast, drawing cartoon faces, like broken limbs are funny. I didn't break legs on holiday. I went to the beach. Swam. Read books. I didn't muffle up in scratchy thermals and stupid brightly coloured puffy anoraks and that year's fashionable sunglasses, and slide up and down hills.

I hated the posh mums and dads who brought their children to school late after the holidays because of skiing. In their Range Rovers, with the ski mounts still on the roof rack.

I hated how people always came back talking about the glühwein, and the food. 'Oh yah, it's basically just an excuse for nosh and plonk. You ski down to this marvellous place for glühwein and tartiflette, and get rarely, rarely pissed and then ski home.'

Have you ever eaten tartiflette? Course you have; you ski. I hate tartiflette – an oily mess of cheesy starch for morons who have worn themselves out in futile kinesis and then frozen themselves solid. Tartiflette is rations, not lunch. And as for raclette – if you can call melted cheese wiped on to a slice of ham a national cuisine, then you must be, well, Swiss.

And I've always hated how people think that skiing is 'sooo much more rewarding than just lying on a beach – I can't bear to just lie about on holiday, I need to have action or I go mad . . .' Really? Well, that's because you are an imbecile. Only the stupid need to be constantly engaged. Only the boring are bored by inactivity. Holidays are for reading. And for reflection. For self-examination. They are when you take quarterly stock of your situation (like a spiritual VAT return), determine where to go next in your life, and prepare to return to it resolved and composed.

They're not for getting so drunk during karaoke night at a Méribel bar that you get lost on the way home and disappear down a crevasse, to be spat out, perfectly preserved, 10,000 years later, as the glacier's eternal turn and slide decides finally to let you go.

The last thing I said to Jules, as I waved him off in his car down the High Street, was: 'Be careful, man, really, it's dangerous.'

And I think he probably just laughed, and told me not to call him 'man'. I don't remember exactly. Either way, he wiped out at speed and came home in a box. And immediately I understood that his death had been unavoidable. His life quickly gathered about it the literal paraphernalia of tragedy. It was clear to me that Jules was always going to die. Was a dead boy walking. And skiing was merely the agent by which it was always going to be brought about.

And so for the next 20 years I had an excuse not to go skiing. I dodged a hundred jollies up a hundred different mountains with the sad tale of how I lost my only pal to skiing, and so wouldn't be able to make it. And it saved me from telling them the real reasons I wouldn't go. Which they wouldn't have understood. The morons.

And then, two years ago, I tried again. I bowed to pressure. I went to Courchevel. I had private lessons every day, just me, the instructor and, of all people, Vincent Cable (don't ask, just let me assure you the old guy is far more confident on the economy than he is on a pair of sliding planks). And I found it a doddle. Red runs in no time. Thought maybe this is OK. Thought maybe I would surrender my whole personality and everything I hold dear, and start going annually.

And then poor Natasha Richardson slipped over on a nursery slope, banged her head and died. She was not killed recklessly flying into a solid object or over a ledge because she wasn't as good as she thought she was (which skiers never, EVER, are), she was killed, most tragically of all, learning.

Learning at 45. Having finally given in to peer pressure after decades of reluctance, perhaps, because she was fed up with people banging on about the glories of skiing all the time, and of feeling left out. It certainly can't be that she had not skied before for lack of opportunity.

Because in a modern middle-class life, believe me, it is *not* going skiing every year that is the really difficult thing.

American Food

The first thing Barack Obama was compelled to do as sworn-in president of the United States was to eat an inaugural luncheon in the Capitol's Statuary Hall – a 100-year-old event hosted by the Joint Congressional Committee on Inaugural Ceremonies and attended by 200 hungry congressmen, Supreme Court judges and other worthies – that looks like it was conceived by an obese nine-year-old on the back of a 48-hour Oreo bender.

Halfway through the main course, I imagine, the most exciting new president since JFK will have suddenly realised the enormity of the task that lies ahead of him. He no doubt reflected, with a weary belch, that this was not what he got into politics for. And when they finally plonked his pudding in front of him, he will have been tempted to lean across to Vice-President Biden and whisper: 'I can't do this, Joe, you take it from here,' before bolting for the door marked Rest Rooms with a suspiciously bulging napkin in his left hand, never to be seen again.

In theory, the menu tied in with the Abraham Lincoln-themed festivities of the day (always beware a themed meal): 'Growing up in the frontier regions of Kentucky and Indiana, the sixteenth president favoured simple foods including root vegetables and wild game,' declared the White House website ahead of the grand scoff. 'As his tastes matured, he became fond of stewed and scalloped oysters. For dessert or a snack, nothing pleased him more than a fresh apple or an apple cake.'

And so, obviously, they prepared a menu that began with many kilos of lobster, scallops, shrimps and black cod boiled in cream and vermouth, then ladled into pastry cases, glazed and baked into pies. Mmm, the joys of simple food.

After the 'fish stew' came a lovely, simple 'Brace of American Birds with Sour Cherry Chutney and Molasses Sweet Potatoes', served, like everything else, on replica china from the Lincoln Administration.

Again, I've looked up the recipe on the White House website (they're terribly proud of this meal and have posted all the recipes in a do-it-yourself-at-home format so that the world's fattest nation can celebrate the renaissance of its democracy in calories – the only language it understands) and discovered that this involved a duck breast slathered with cherry and raisin jam sharing a (replica Lincolnian) plate with a pheasant breast that had been stuffed with, and I quote, 'football-shaped patties' of a rice-and-canned-chicken-soup concoction I would hesitate to put out for the foxes.

I mean, 'football-shaped'?

What sort of a national cuisine measures out its ingredients in footballs? The rest of the world uses tablespoons and cups but in America, hell no, we gonna use a football of rice! We gonna let our wide receivers go and we gonna throw that damn lunch for a touchdown!

It's all so giant and sweet and sickly. And as if that wasn't enough, the birds were served with a dish of 'molasses whipped sweet potatoes', involving these already very sweet vegetables being baked and then mashed with – wait for it – brown sugar, molasses, orange juice and maple syrup. Talk about your five portions. This was food for a nation of babies. No wonder presidents do so much running. Any less than five miles a day and within a year Obama won't even fit in the Oval Office.

And then after a meal that already had more sugar in it than your average wedding cake, the guests at Statuary Hall were expected to eat an apple sponge cake served with vanilla ice cream and a cinnamon sauce based on, and again I quote: 'caramel sauce (store bought)'.

The tragedy of American cooking is that it just can't get a grip of 'simple, elegant and smart'. America is fantastic at chow. It leads the world in low-key catering. It is great at barbecues, fried chicken, burgers, sweet pies and soft drinks. It is kiddy heaven. But it can't do grown-up.

Bashfully imitating what it thinks of as European sophistication, upscale American cuisine always overelaborates. It puts wetback waiters in rented tuxes and serves clam chowder from silver tureens, it flames things at the table and always puts a lobster on the side. It makes no choices, it does everything at once: surf'n'turf, pancakes and bacon, marshmallows and yams.

No pheasant needs its breast stuffed, no duck needs cherry chutney. No lobster truly revels in the company of cod, shrimps, scallops, vermouth and cream. To be honest, and this is a funny time to say it, but I'd much rather have been invited to a Bush luncheon of barbecued pork chops and Bud.

I have no doubt that Abraham Lincoln's simple meals of fresh sea scallops, root vegetables and wild game were absolutely delicious. And I wish the guardians of modern American presidential cuisine had had the confidence to replicate them exactly, without all the modernising and fannying around.

American upscale dining is in a parlous state, but I guess nobody is better placed to put it right than the new Messiah whom this terrible, terrible meal was designed to celebrate.

Not long after the inauguration I found myself, by chance, in the Southern part of the United States and thinking about its food once again. I found that, like most of the paradoxes enshrined in its bright-eyed little constitution, America's food, for the most part, offers the illusion of choice and democracy while providing, in reality, a single, unending, fascistically regimented product that runs counter to everything we climbed out of the sea and grew heads for.

I ate hotdogs in the South. I ate cheese-dogs, slaw-dogs, chilli-dogs, chicken-dogs, fish-dogs, veggie-dogs, double-dogs and choc-dogs. I ate them at baseball games (where the match-day programme listed 48 different kinds of food available at 120 outlets in the stadium), and at the roadside and at a famous restaurant called Varsity that was celebrating its 75th anniversary.

And I ate pulled pork with vinegar sauce. I ate it 'tailgating' in the car park at a college football game, at a fund-raising barbecue for a Republican senator, and in tacquerias and upscale old-school eateries. I ate fried chicken and Cuban sandwiches, burgers, beans, black-eye peas and field-peas with fake eyes, turnip greens and tacos and 80 types of fried potato. Fried chicken, fried fish, fried ribs . . . and everything, every goddam mouthful (with the exception of a home-cooked pot-roast, a picnic and one great restaurant called Bacchanalia) tasted the same.

The food in the Land of the Free is no different from the food in rural Ukraine in the darkest hours of Stalinism. It's just brighter coloured and there's more of it.

Ask for eggs and they ask how you want them. Say 'fried' and they say 'fried how?', say 'over easy' and they say 'regular, large, extra large, brown, white, duck, chicken or ptarmigan, free-range, organic or farm fresh, whites only or yolks too, salt or no salt?' And then they bring you the plate and you wonder why they bothered to ask if they were going to put the eggs on a waffle and cover them with maple syrup and grits.

Grits are the sick of an infant child who has been fed sweetcorn too early in the weaning process. But they are the very mortar of soul food. In fact, they may be the very mortar of mortar. (The real answer to how an American wants his eggs, of course, is 'hatched, raised to maturity on a diet of GM corn and steroids, killed, dunked in flour and salt, fried until it resembles no more a chicken than a wind-eroded sandstone gargoyle, and served with fries.)

Two weeks of salt, fat and sugar left me fat as an off-season oyster, happy/irritable (depending on that moment's blood-sugar status), bloated and hungry, slightly greasy, full of wind, unwilling to travel anywhere except by car, disinclined to read, preferring to lie farting in front of the television, bored by sporting events with pauses of more than eight seconds between goals, uncomfortable in anything but jogging pants and trainers, slack-jawed from a lack of chewing (the food being soft enough to ingest straight from fork), so tending to drawl my words and avoid long or difficult ones, and too dependent on consumption and too obsessed with volume and cheapness to have any time for the contemplation of liberal thought.

I was an American. I lay smudged across the seat of my SUV with a three-litre plastic cup of Coke, and cried: 'Nuke Iraq, lock up the wetbacks, lynch the faggots, shoot the gynaecologists, send money to Jesus and bring me a jumbo chilli-dog and a root-beer float. And get me a voting form and point my writing hand to where it says "Schwarzenegger".'

Dancing

When *The Times* reported that Britain is in the 'bottom third of European nations' for physical activity levels, I thought it was a very apposite use of the word 'bottom'. We are in the 'bottom' third: the group of European nations which is made up mostly of bottoms.

Holland, Estonia and Germany, on the other hand, are in the 'top' third, and their people consist almost entirely of heads, shoulders and biceps. Croatia, Romania and Finland, at Nos 14, 15 and 16, are in the 'middle' third, a little soft around the belly, a bit midriffy, but still just about holding it together.

And then there's us at No. 21, and then Cyprus, Turkey, Sweden, Italy ... the great arse nations. The countries whose inhabitants never exercise at all and are thus, for the most part, nothing more than a giant pair of buttocks with a pair of cheap trainers and a hat.

And so the Health Secretary has decided to get us all exercising. At this news we all yawn, stretch, groan and file it away with the 'five portions' farrago under futile government initiatives designed to deflect attention from inadequate education, craven indulgence of the giant food conglomerates that have been poisoning us for years, and the fact that the only strategy they've come up with to keep disaffected schoolchildren out of trouble is to fill their mouths so full of Monster Munch and Coke they won't have anywhere to put the crack pipe, and will be too obese for underage sex.

But the minister, ahead of the 2012 Olympics, has no plans to get us running and jumping and throwing things in the traditional sense. Nor are there plans to get us playing a bit of cricket. As for tennis, we're leaving that to Andy Murray. What he wants us to do is dance. And so he has appointed Arlene Phillips, the rejected *Strictly Come Dancing* judge, as his dance czar, along with the failed contestant Lisa Snowdon, to organise mass, indiscriminate dancing.

Dance, the last cultural resort of the bona fide imbecile. The party pastime of people who are too stupid to talk. The perverse repetitive jiggling, mostly when intoxicated, of proper, old-fashioned idiots, who consider it an entertainment to resign their decisions about bodily movement to the group, subsume their individual identities to the horde, and simply spasm to the throb, throb, throb of the pill-befuddled loser at the front with the very loud gramophone.

Never, as a younger man, did I feel more alone than sitting in a nightclub, on my own at a table, keeping watch over the drinks and phones and bags and coats, while my friends went to twitch involuntarily in response to a noise coming out of boxes mounted on the wall. I felt like the only dissenter at a Nuremberg rally, the only one stepping back and saying, 'Wait, hang on, this is wrong'. It would be just as bad at weddings, birthday parties and bar mitzvahs. Worse, even, because you are usually insulting someone by declining. I am revolted by obesity, God knows. But I am revolted even more by dancing.

'We have to set up centres,' Ms Phillips gushed, like some warzone paramedic risking her life to organise a network of field hospitals for napalmed children. 'We have to find places where people can just walk to get where they can dance. We have to make it part of people's daily lives.'

What a horrific thought. It puts one immediately in mind of the St Vitus' dance epidemic that began in Germany in 1347 and soon spread across medieval Europe: an unexplained plague of hysterical dancing, night and day, passed on, apparently, by the mere witnessing of the event. It was the 14th-century equivalent of those terrifying dance happenings in stations and airports where thousands of brain-dead freaks with iPods suddenly start dancing silently to the same song.

In the 14th century such people were assumed to have been possessed by the Devil. And even today I think that is a pretty fair diagnosis. When I see a kid even tapping his foot to an MP3 tune on the bus, my thoughts turn immediately to the ducking stool.

Sure, we must tackle the obesity crisis, the fecklessness disease, the podginess pandemic, the megabloat timebomb, call it what you will. But please God don't let's leave it to a couple of foot-tapping old dears no longer required by a reality dance show. What a hellish chain of thought must have gone on in the health office: 'What shall we do with Arlene and Lisa now that junk television doesn't want them any more? Ooh, I know, bring them to the heart of government. That'll get the moronic, telly-doped, witless, couch potato peasantry to sit up and take notice.'

If they can sit up. Probably they'll just have their council-appointed £100,000-a-year specialist obesity carer raise one of their eyebrows for them, fart, and go back to sleep.

Arlene Phillips, for heaven's sake. I mean, she looks good for 106, I'll grant you, but she has used Botox, hankers publicly after a gastric band and admits: 'I know I will have a facelift eventually.' What sense, what depth, what humanity. From the waist up she'll be mostly polythene.

Is that what the health secretary secretly wants us to do: liposuck, Botox and tummy tuck our way to a higher spot on the list? Will Arlene be put in charge of that, too? Will she combine her dance czar duties with being the government's Cosmetic Surgery Kommandant? His Plastic Pope?

Perhaps it would be best to give her a peerage, like Alan Sugar, so she can get in there and get the Lords hopping about to some preposterous tweenybop girl band caterwauling. Give her an office, stick 'Botox'n'Groovin' Minister' on the door, and wait for the votes to roll in. Then maybe ennoble that Liverpudlian builder who won the first series of *Big Brother*, Craig I think his name was, and make him housing czar. And that hairy Scottish woman who failed to win the singing show would make an ideal prime minister – she is the spit and image of Gordon Brown and, like him, knows just how to fall to bits when your one big chance finally comes.

Offering a model for her mass danceathons, Ms Phillips says: 'In China, where in open spaces people join in and take t'ai chi with the masses, it's there, it's available.'

Great idea, Arlene, old girl. Let's take our lead from an overpopulated dictatorship where people gather in public to do exactly as they are told, partly because there is nothing else to do, and partly because if they don't they'll be shot. George Orwell said: 'If you want a picture of the future, imagine a boot stamping on a human face – for ever.' But only because he did not dare entertain the nightmare of 'a boot dancing to some cool tunes in public'.

I'm no fan of the fat, but I will defend to the death (or until one of them sits on me) their right to be free. I will not kowtow to the communism of dance.

People Who Bag Sun-Loungers with Bad Books

The Colombe d'Or in St-Paul de Vence is one of the most beautiful hotels in the world. Hunkered low in the Alpes-Maritimes, in the lee of the beautiful medieval perched village, it has a modern art collection to make your eyes water, the most beautiful garden restaurant in Europe, and an air of relaxed, bourgeois geniality that cannot be bettered.

The problem is with the pool. Not with the beautiful location, for the climber-clad walls, yew hedge and sea views are unparalleled, the sculpture opposite the diving board inspired. The waitress service quite gorgeous and the pool itself green and limpid (if a little warm).

The problem is with the unseemly practice by which the idle millionaires who populate the place go scuttling to the pool on their way to breakfast, and leave books or hats on the sun loungers they think that they may require later. Some bag a pair at either end of the pool, to be well positioned to rotate with the sun, like some fat, tanned, Ferrari-toting sunflower.

Personally, I just won't be a part of such grasping, antisocial solipsism and choose to breakfast at my leisure then take my chances by the pool. Yesterday morning I had a nice swim and, finding no lounger unbagged, obviously had to lie on a pre-bagged one.

'You can't do that!' said an onlooking guest as I picked up his neighbour's book and flung it aside to make room for my wet arse.

'I most certainly can,' I said. 'The geezer's tried to bag his spot with a David Baldacci. I'm not going to stand here soaking wet to make room for a Baldacci.'

I have since developed in my mind a hierarchy of lounger-bagging enforceability based on literary merit. Later that day I happily gave way to the new J.M. Coetzee novel, because I happen to have packed a copy myself.

I have also respected a dog-eared American paperback of Saul Bellow's *Herzog*, two Ian McEwans, three books in French (on the basis that the reader is either making a damn fine effort to get in the local spirit or is actually French, which is quite a novelty round here) and, after hesitation, a biography of Harry Redknapp.

But, ye gods, the Dan Browns, Stieg Larssons, Stephenie Meyers and James Pattersons I have hurled aside to take some sun. One Kathy Reichs, I'm afraid, even disappeared over a stone wall and into the valley below.

I will not give way to books by celebrities either, nor political biographies of anyone born after the First World War, nor faux-lit drivel such as Yann Martel, Aravind Adiga, Mark Haddon, Audrey Niffenegger or Khaled Hosseini – dreary kids' yarns given prizes because thicko celebrity judges who wished they had never agreed to the job managed to finish them.

It's a minefield, but I've managed to get a tan. So this year, if you're holidaying where sun space is at a premium and bed-bagging is indulged, be careful what you read.

Feet

How I dread the arrival of summer and the excuse it provides for people to get their feet out, presenting them for our delectation in flip-flops, sandals and open-toed mules at the first hint of a break in the clouds.

Why? Heat rises (or hadn't you heard?). There is absolutely no reason why your feet, way down there at the bottom, should, in shoes and socks, get any hotter in summer than in winter. Your top half, sure, but not your feet. And your feet are ugly, bone ugly. They should stay under wraps.

Men's feet, in particular, make me squirm and gag: the mottled colouring, the sparse hair, the little toe that has been crushed into the one next to it over the years so that it has turned and bent and cuddles up against it now, sadly, as if trying to spoon an unwilling lover, the yellowed, cracked toenails, and the fully blackened one on the right biggy from toe-punting a goalpost 14 years ago. How can bringing these out in public be considered acceptable?

The sight of such a foot in flip-flops, walking on an urban street, in a shop, or on a bus, is just so wrong, the flappy plastic sole going slap, slap, slap against the sweaty arch. And sometimes you see people in flip-flops on the Underground. Seriously, aren't they worried that somebody will stamp on their toes – either accidentally or, if the somebody happens to be me, deliberately?

And I am no big fan of 'style' sandals either, not the Jesus ones (the only time Jesus got it really wrong was in the shoe shop), nor the shiny Italian type with big lateral straps that some men seem to think it is acceptable to pair with shorts and a suit jacket and go to work in.

Worst of all are those preposterous action sandals in which men's gnarly white hoofs are strapped on to a black foam float with so many cross straps and bits of Velcro that it's basically a ventilated rambling boot – the ultimate *Guardian* reader's summer shoe. I saw Ranulph Fiennes advertising them once and, having previously rather admired the man, decided that henceforth I would regard every toe taken from him by frostbite as a blow struck for decency and good taste.

Nor are women's feet much better. They are usually smaller, at least, which is something. For less is most definitely more. And they are sometimes better kept, even pedicured, to make a place for nail varnish.

Oh, how women love to paint a toe. For nine months of the year they can only slap brightly coloured chemicals over their eyes, lips, nose, cheeks, hair and fingernails. Summer opens up ten new little canvasses.

But they do it only when the sun first comes out and then very quickly lose interest in maintenance so that, as the nail grows, the painted bit gets smaller and travels towards the end of the foot, leaving a rough patch of sparse, unpainted keratin behind, which looks really slutty and grim.

And what's with all these women who don't really have a toenail on their little toe, just the merest sliver poking out in the middle, who then try and paint the toe around it to make it look bigger? Please don't do that, I've just had breakfast.

But then all women's open shoes are revolting. Those strappy mules where the sole rolls out of the end of a wide, asymmetric toe-hole so that the shoe looks like it is vomiting toes. Toes that are all pointing to an imaginary origin just in front of the middle toe because of being crammed into closed, pointy shoes all winter. And heels all red and covered in Elastoplasts because in early summer the bare skin is not yet used to the rub of the strap.

Worst of all are these quasi-bondage (or 'slapper') shoes of which Louis Vuitton does a version called the 'Spicy', which involve a vertiginous heel sloping down to a two-inch platform and the foot tied in with all sorts of ribbons and chains. I think it's meant to be a nod to fetish, but the effect is to make the wearer (who is paying maybe a grand a pair) look as desperate and slaggy as a pole dancer, while at the same time reminding us of the horrors of ancient Chinese foot-binding.

Why a woman would want to draw attention to her nasty little bunioned trotters on a night out, I just cannot imagine. I doubt they do. It's just that these are shoes designed by men who are not into women, and cannot bear to think too much about any part of them more intimate than their feet.

And it's not just shoes. All sorts of terrible things happen to our clothes in hot weather. Fat people, for example, suddenly start wearing trousers that come down only to mid-calf.

Challenged, they will say that these are more comfortable than full trousers. But of all the parts of a fat man's body that might be uncomfortable in clothes, you wouldn't imagine that his ankles were a major issue. How uncomfortable is the bottom of a trouser? It's trousers with no arse you'd think a fat person would want to wear, and shirts with slits for his bingo wings, and jumpers with a tyre-sized hole in the front to let his gut hang out, all cool and comfy.

I abhor skinny men, too, mind. Those horrible crew-cut lads who stride around topless in town, in their jeans and box-fresh trainers, alabaster-skinned with little pink nipples and pointy elbows pumping jerkily, like that's an okay way for a gentleman to be seen in public. But only here, only in Britain. In hot countries, never. And they're always tattooed. It gets worse every year.

You forget about it over the winter, when people are all nicely muffled in coats and scarves. And then there's a flicker of sun and in parks all over the country the unwashed hordes strip to their nuts to reveal meaningless symbols and foreign alphabets carved all over their skin.

Swimming at the Hampstead lido the other day, I felt like Captain Cook landing for the first time in Polynesia – the only unpainted man for thousands of miles. People gaped in awe at the aggressiveness of my undoodled carapace. I swear, so ubiquitous have tattoos become, so much the uniform of every naked Briton, that unpainted skin now seems rebellious and exotic. Being untattooed is the new tattoo.

A man sitting next to me by the pool had a large one on his arm of a man sitting on the toilet. When I asked him why, he said 'it seemed like a good idea at the time', and I tried desperately to imagine what sort of a time that might have been.

Another, a large, hard man apparently carved from teak, had 'French Foreign Legion' written on his chest. I asked him if he had really been in the bloodthirsty Legion of which one hears such terrible things, and he leant towards me and growled: 'It would be a f***ing stupid tattoo to 'ave if I 'adn't, wouldn't it?' And so I packed up my things and went quietly home.

Poetry

There was a brief flurry of excitement about poetry in the summer of 2009. Not about the poems themselves, of course, God forbid, but about the poets. First, Carol Ann Duffy was appointed Poet Laureate, the first woman to land the job – Wahaaay! Then the other big job in versifying, the Oxford professorship, was mired in scandal by the multimedia slandering and subsequent withdrawal from the race of poor old Derek Walcott, who had only hoped, in the tradition of Benjamin Zephaniah, to be rejected as Oxford's Professor of Poetry fairly, at the voting stage, in favour of whichever white person left in the ballot could spell his or her own name.

That post, ultimately, also went to a woman, Ruth Padel. Slightly smaller 'wahay'. Boring now. But then interesting again, as she resigned, having been implicated in the Walcott scandal.

All very exciting, very public stuff. But I think that in the commotion the core of the thing was lost. The ball was dropped. The single eternal truth at the heart of English poetry was forgotten.

Which is that nobody gives a toss about it.

Nobody cares. Nobody at all. Nooooooobody. Who is the outgoing Oxford poetry professor? Come on, come on . . . Wrong! Seamus Heaney was ages ago. It's Christopher Ricks, who, although he is a great critic, is not even a poet. And who was it before Heaney? Don't worry, I've no idea either! And, since Heaney took up the post in 1989, whoever the hell came before him was in the job while I was actually at Oxford, doing an English degree. That's how much of a toss we give.

The English love of poetry is a mirage, one of the great national cons. It's up there with Beefeaters, morris dancing and shortbread – just another thing that was never important except to a very small number of people, never relevant, never mattered, but is clung onto nowadays because otherwise what would they write on tea towels?

Perhaps you disagree. Perhaps you are, yourself, a poetry lover. Course you are, dear. What English girl isn't? OK then, what is your favourite poem? The one you know best, love most, can recite in full and have a vague idea what it's about.

It's one you did at school, isn't it? Probably for GCSE or O level. Unless it's Kipling's 'If', in which case you bought *The Times* only because the newsagent had run out of the *Daily Mail*, and you didn't go to school at all.

You see, we all want to believe we love poetry. We all have a stock of poems, half-learnt in school – a couple of Shakespeare sonnets, a line or two of Wordsworth, bits of Chaucer, the last line of 'Ozymandias' and the first line of 'The Love Song of J. Alfred Prufrock' – that we roll out at parties and use to persuade ourselves that we are part of the great tradition. But it's all a fraud.

We love poems that we were taught in school because they do not scare us. We were told what they are about long ago by people who were paid to tell us, back when our little memories could hold on to stuff like that. But who can be bothered with a new poem? Even a new poem by an old poet? All those words that may mean more than they appear to mean, all that obfuscation, no story to speak of, no jokes, only meandering sentences that quite soon have you staring out of the window and wondering what's on the telly . . .

We love the idea of our poetic history in part because we don't have much in the way of painters or composers compared with our European neighbours, and cleave to the idea that England gave poetry to the world. So we wear the old stuff as a badge ('oh, I loooove Keats'), but we don't even reread the poems we do like, and end up generally with nothing but the same dusty old one-liners growing foxed and mottled on our mental shelves.

On the day that *The Times* went big on the Ruth Padel story, for example, two of the paper's biggest-hitting critics, Richard Morrison and Andrew Billen, chose to adorn their columns (on unrelated subjects) with the same allusion to John Donne's line about no man being an island. A staggering coincidence? Or just evidence that that lone gag is all that has really survived of Donne's work, even in the memories of writers?

On the same day, this paper's leading article on Padelgate opened with Shelley's line about 'the unacknowledged legislators of the world'. And that's no coincidence either because, apart from the aforementioned bit of 'Ozymandias', it is about all that anyone nowadays can remember of Shelley.

If you want to know how little we care about poetry, then you might want to bear in mind that of the 150,000 Oxford graduates who were eligible to vote for the poetry professor, only 426 bothered. That's a turnout of less than 0.3 per cent. At its lowest ebb, the American electorate is 150 times more interested in choosing its president than that. And it's even worse when you bear in mind that that was 0.3 per cent of an electorate drawn from the 0.25 per cent of Britons most likely to give a damn.

Staggering, really, that it got in the papers at all. Except that what really got in the papers was a row between a woman and a West Indian man over the spectre of unwilling sex. Which is all that was unusual about what was, in the end, just another disagreement between poets.

But, of course, disagreement between poets has always interested us far more than poetry itself. The big questions in poetry have never been about lexicon, syntax or metre, but about personality: who was Shakespeare? Who stabbed Christopher Marlowe? Did Ted Hughes drive two wives to suicide, or did he just happen to like mad girls? Did Philip Larkin die a virgin? Did the ladies love Byron despite his club foot or because of it? How short was Pope? (I swear to God, more people – Oxford graduates included – will tell you Pope's height to the nearest inch than can give you three consecutive words from the *Dunciad*.)

Maybe it's just that modern poetry is rubbish. And maybe that's because, as *The Times* observed in a leader on the subject, poetry doesn't really pay. The position of Oxford poetry professor, for example, comes with a miserable £6,901. Padel would have done better to get a job flipping burgers at McDonald's.

Current thinking on MPs and teachers is that if only we could pay them a bit more, maybe we'd get better ones. Perhaps the same is true of poets. Perhaps the time has come to throw some real money at them. At the time of all these poetry shenanigans, I was appearing at the Hay-on-Wye literary festival where poets come from all over Britain in the hope of making a few extra quid, but are utterly ignored while people queue round the block for Alistair McGowan and Ben Fogle.

And here's a funny thing: you'd have thought that people at the Hay Festival, above all people, might just be interested in a reading by the Oxford Professor of Poetry. But they weren't. I know this because there was a reading by Ruth Padel one afternoon, widely advertised as an appearance by the new Oxford Professor of Poetry, for which tickets were selling like cold sick. You couldn't give them away.

Then she resigned, and the event sold out in minutes. Which goes to show that your average literary Briton will pay good money only to go and see a person performing who is absolutely and totally *not* the Oxford Professor of Poetry.

Museums

There was outrage in Austria, as I'm sure you remember, when it was reported that Beyoncé had ducked out of a planned trip to the famous Albertina museum in Vienna and sent along a look-alike to feign interest in the exhibits and pose for photographs with Dr Klaus Albrecht Schröder, the director of the museum, while she went shopping.

The local tabloids, *Osterreich* and *Heute*, were both furious with the pop star and quoted a museum spokesman as having said: 'What a cheek! We were a little doubtful yesterday, but weren't really sure.'

And it *could* have been quite tricky, I guess, for a nation so historically racist that it got behind Kurt Waldheim's presidential campaign only *after* he was exposed as a former SS officer, to cast doubt on the authenticity of a black pop star who was apparently standing there in the flesh.

I can just imagine, as the fake Beyoncé smiled and waved, the mutterings among Viennese bystanders of: 'Hmm, she doesn't look zo gut as in ze video for Boodylicious; I'd svear to Gott her ass is bigger, but, you know, zey all look sort of ze same . . .'

Still, whether or not one is a big fan of the Austrians, it does look rather terrible that this screeching, dim-witted diva, who has got rich peddling formulaic ditties to the iPod generation, should have snubbed a museum that houses some of the greatest art in the world. And I did, initially, think to myself: 'Bloody hell, woman, couldn't you cease your moronic wailing for just a minute to think about something higher? Don't you think it would have been a good example to set to your knuckle-dragging teenage fan base at least to have pretended to be interested in the Albertina's vast collection of paintings by the world's most famous artists?'

But then I thought, hang on, who am I kidding? I would have done exactly the same as Beyoncé (who, it later transpired, had not even promised to show up in the first place – it was all just a HILARIOUS hoax by an Austrian radio station). Who in the world would *not* rather stay in bed than trog round some dreary art gallery? Who in the world would not, if they had the option, send along a lookalike every time they were faced with an impending museum visit?

Does anyone really look forward to milling among the hordes of crisp-scoffing nine-year-olds, moody art students sulkily sketching the fire extinguisher, fiftysomething vegans in bow-ties on blind dates with someone they met on *The Guardian*'s 'Soul Mates' website and general assorted old perverts smelling faintly of Murray Mints pressing their noses up against glass cases of ancient crap donated by someone who looted it illegally in the first place?

If I could find anyone who looked half like me and was in need of paid work, hell, I'd never see the inside of a museum again. And I wouldn't stop at museums. If I were lucky enough to have a lookalike on my payroll I would wheel him out whenever I was staring down the barrel of an invitation to the ballet, too. And he would also go to every opera, play and classical concert I was daft enough to have accepted an invitation to months before, on account of having failed to observe the old 'never say "yes" to anything three months away that you would be dreading if it were tomorrow' rule.

Never again would I sit in some silent hall on a stone-hard, creaking seat, busting for a wee and wondering if we were past the halfway mark yet. I would be at home with my feet up, slurping a takeaway korma and watching the football while people ogled the sparsely bearded, slightly squinty-looking dark fellow in the floral shirt sitting in the front row, and were pretty certain that Giles Coren had showed up as promised.

And if it worked at public gatherings then I would extend my lookalike's range. Ersatz Giley would soon find his summer blighted by country weddings that I had been too cowardly to say no to. He would go to summer drinks in the next-door neighbour's garden, he would yodel 'Happy Birthday!' at cringe-making surprise parties and he would always be delighted to do a small unpaid item about bean farming on 'You and Yours'.

Having a lookalike is surely the greatest perk available to the successful human. To be in more than one place at once (with the paradoxical boon of being, effectively, nowhere) is the dream of every man. Hiring a roster of facsimile selves is practically the first thing a dictator does on coming to power (just after killing all the politicians), and now I understand why.

Saddam Hussein, for example, had several lookalikes. I bet he never had to go to the ballet. Castro had them, Kim Jong Il has them (basically any old Korean washerwoman qualifies) and, of course, Hitler had a whole team of men who looked exactly like him, sounded like him and said all the same things as him. And they were all, of course, extremely popular in Austria.

Hotels

The difference between a good restaurant and a good hotel is that in a good restaurant you expect to find high standards of service and product, decent value, and then also originality, flair, wit and sophistication. Whereas in a good hotel you just hope it won't be awful.

I go to hotels quite a lot, overnighting after a restaurant review somewhere, or attempting to build a couple of out-of-town write-ups into a jolly weekend of some sort, and, honestly, it is so dispiriting.

It goes without saying that provincial city-centre chain hotels (called things like CheapSleep and Bog'n'Bed), and those slightly cheaper versions of them that cluster on ring-road round-abouts (called CheapSleepQuick and Bog'n'Bed-Budget) are too depressing even to commit suicide in. ('A doorknob strong enough to hang yourself from? That'll be a £10 supplement, I'm afraid.')

A couple of steps up from there you arrive at those ones with a restaurant-of-sorts (open from 7 p.m. till 8 p.m.), where regional sales managers can eat a £17 fish cake made of pipe-lagging and pilchard with two pints of warm lager, and then retire to a polyester cubicle for feats of lonely onanism with husband-of-the-Home-Secretary-level cable pornography for £6/hour.

And then, if you start paying £100 a night or more, you might get a restaurant which carries the name of a chef you've seen on telly but is equally awful, a gym containing one broken exercise bike and a yoga mat with a gruesome sticky patch in the middle, and one or two staff who don't have visible boils. There's a weeny kettle all clogged with limescale in a drawer, which can just about make enough hot water to fill a cup and a half, and some old, stale sachets of Lipton's with an invitation to call reception for fresh milk, which you do, and then wait while your stale, weak tea goes cold, and then another half an hour, and then they bring you an ironing board.

But I'm not talking about those. I'm talking about the places where rooms start at £200/night and head up into the stratosphere. The ones with Michelin-starred restaurants and beautiful photos on their websites of Palladian architecture and rolling fields, and lakes, and beautiful maids, and a vast swimming pool.

These always turn out to be bang on an A-road carrying trans-national freight all day and night, above whose rumble you struggle to make your complaints about the whining, not-cold fridge and armpit-smelling pillows heard, and in the presence of which sleep is no more than a tasteless joke.

They always appear to have only three staff (two mute Slavs and a hunchbacked, drooling thing that was no doubt drummed out of its village with broom handles and saucepans when one too many cats went missing in the dead of night), so that if someone is checking in a new arrival at the front desk there will be nobody to man the bar on the other side of the house, and you have to prowl the corridors looking for someone to mix you a bad gin and tonic, poking your head into empty kitchens and scary, 'staff only' store cupboards in the search for life.

The Palladian architecture turns out to typify only the small main hotel, with four lovely rooms available to honeymooners who book three years in advance, but not the vast, freezing, 100-room annexe they've put you in. The rolling fields and lake are an hour's drive away, the swimming pool is only eight feet long and is closed for maintenance, and the maids turn out to be downloaded stills from YouPorn (which cannot, incidentally, be accessed from your room because the broadband connection is down until October).

It's true the restaurant has a Michelin star, but the room is a morgue. The place where pelmets go to die. In the gloomy light sit three dozen of the wealthiest local reptiles, coughing. You are forced to drink a bad cocktail ('Sorry, we only have Beefeater') in a terrifying lounge and order from the sofa, then proceed through to where your fancily stacked mousseline of something is developing the texture of elderly human skin, and the whole place has the carrion whiff of truffle oil. At least, you hope it's truffle oil.

Next day, there's nothing to do. They recommend a walk to a local pub and after an hour sidling single-file down the edge of a dual carriageway you come to a shabby Wetherspoon's which is closed for the local skittles tournament. You walk back to your room, run a lukewarm bath, and lie in it reading a three-day-old paper as the sinking water level, thanks to the not-quite-fitting plug, gradually exposes more and more of your cold body.

And then, finally, because you must check out within minutes of finishing breakfast on Sunday (and don't even think about asking for your eggs nice and soft), you go home.

And you swear, to the sorry gods who made you, never to go away again.

Cloning

I do love a good mouse cloning. They've done it again now with the production of a mouse that is the daughter of two mothers. And they are actual, bona fide biological mothers. This was not two lesbian mice living in a co-operative housing project in Dalston, claiming nine hundred quid a week 'gender-readjustment' benefit, and badgering the little mouse adoption agencies to let them adopt even though little mouse rightwingers thinks it's unnatural.

Until relatively recently, same-sex mouse couples did not know that they wanted to bring up families, but it will come as a great relief to gay rodents the world over to know that their procreative dreams are no longer at the whim of some homophobic mouse counsellor who wants to give the litter of 14 on which they have set their heart to boring old Mickey and Minnie, the bourgeois heteros who live in the gap behind the fridge.

Yes, mouse cloning. Surely the very zenith of the biologist's art. Were I some biogenetic megaboffin you would not catch me farting about all day demanding £20 million from Government to set up anti-biological warfare units or trying to solve world hunger by crossing rice with orphans (to create an underclass that eats itself). Oh no, I would be in a nice warm corner of the lab listening to Capital Radio and doing hilarious things to mice. Like those fellows who cloned a huge human ear on to a mouse. Genius. Except that an eye would have been more spooky. Or a willy. No, a willy would be funniest on a grass snake.

That's what I'd have done if I had spent ten years at Cambridge doing three consecutive doctorates. What, I ask you, is the point of a science education if you can't do things like that?

Except that I think mouse cloning is not what the top boffins do. The swottiest ones get swept off early to make weapons of mass destruction to sell to foreign despots so that later on in life they can have a nice long sabbatical in the desert looking for them. It is only the skivers and bunkers who end up cloning mice. That's why I would have ended up a mouse cloner if I'd got past O level with my sciences.

I can just see myself dozing at my microscope after a beery lunch when a tennis ball thrown by a workmate, which has missed our little basketball hoop, hits me on the head and I wake up and realise that it is pushing five and we haven't done anything all afternoon. The boss will be round in a minute and all I've got to show for my working day is a lot of personal e-mails, a half-read copy of *Heat* magazine and a sweaty Carlsberg headache. What can I do in ten minutes to make the day retrospectively worth while?

I know: quick, clone a mouse. Shall I stick an ear on him? Been done. See if he gets cancer from a diet of Big Macs and fags? No time. Christ, that's the boss at the door now. Think, think. Yes, two girl mice, bit of parthenogenesis, wham bam, first mammalian child of lesbo parents. Done.

Phew. Nobel prize in the post. Lovely job.

In the aftermath of this astonishing breakthrough, Thursday's *Daily Mail* managed to dig up some tub-thumping foetus-fancier who thought that it signalled the beginning of the end for the male sex. Professor Jack Scarisbrick (very possibly a real person) of the anti-abortion charity Life declared: 'It is barbaric. It's not the way forward for a civilised society. It's a stepping stone to the fatherless child and the ultimate sop to militant feminists – soon they will be saying it is their 'right' to have a fatherless child.'

These militant feminists, eh? Lucky we've got the *Daily Mail* and *Life* to keep an eye on them. And I don't think these are mouse feminists they are talking about, either. I think they are talking about real women in dungarees, with beaded hair and placards.

But just because the *Daily Mail* is scaremongering about it, it doesn't mean that it couldn't happen. Men may well be obsolete within a generation. Can we imagine a world with no men? Who would clean the windows? Who would teach carpentry to the thick kids in schools? Who would do the muggings? Who would have the fist fights that need to be had over precedence at traffic lights? Who would kick their pants into the air after taking them off at night and catch them behind their head? Who would keep his old school cricket bat in the cupboard under the stairs even though he hasn't played in 40 years and occasionally take it out to practise his forward defensive in the bedroom mirror? Who would clone the mice?

Any man you ask would admit that obsolescence is an ambition we have held for years. From the Industrial Revolution onwards man has worked towards nothing less than his own superannuation. That's why we love feminism. We are tired now. If women suddenly want to do all the work, earn all the money, do all the driving and the warmongering and the boxing and the building and the writing, then that is marvellous. It is the very best 'thank you' imaginable for all the years of schlepping around after you.

And if you think you can take it one step farther, and arrange it so that we don't even have to exist (you ladies will find, once you get your head round what we chaps call 'philosophy', that existence is the most painful thing of all), well then, bring it on. Until then, I am one man who would be very proud to be a mouse.

School Subjects

Every generation of schoolchildren needs a new set of wacko principles imposed on its education by the generation of middle-aged pedagogical wonks whose own education was screwed up by the wacko ideas of the previous lot; and who is to say that the middle-aged pedagogical wonks of tomorrow will not look back with a grateful and teary eye on the pedagogical wonks of today, who have (in Sir Jim Rose's interim report for the Schools Secretary) proposed the abolition of 'subjects' altogether?

Subjects were always a bum idea, if you ask me. A bourgeois construct inclined to restrict rather than expand the opportunities for self-fulfilment. For example, I was stigmatised for my entire school career by the utterly misguided notion that I was 'bad at maths', a hastily applied and grossly inaccurate label that stuck with me quite unfairly from the age of 5 for very nearly ten years until I was, ooh, 18 or 19.

Had there, however, been no such thing as 'maths', so that I was merely 'bad at that count-y thing we do on Tuesdays and Wednesdays before lunch and twice on Friday afternoon', then I might have been OK. Although I grant it would be a bore for such mathematicians as John Horton Conway or Grigory Perelman to have to be introduced, at parties say, as the greatest 'doer of that Tuesday, Wednesday and Friday count-y thing since Pythagoras'.

In recent years, it has been fashionable to scoff at Francis Fukuyama's announcement in 1992 of the 'end of history', pointing out that the fall of communism and the death of ideology has by no means spelt the end of material progress but merely moved the diodes around which historical forces polarise.

Now, however, we can clearly see that Fukuyama didn't mean history was over, per se, just that it was changing its name to 'Human Social and Environmental Understanding'.

It is, however, the end of geography (it will also, confusingly, be called Human Social and Environmental Understanding) that will cause the greatest upset, for if there is no geography then what on earth will the PE master teach as his indoor subject? (I mean, come on, you can't teach Human Social and Environmental Understanding wearing a tracksuit, now can you?)

I was reasonably OK at English, and proud of it. It is, after all, the only meaningful thing to be good at. Being good at French or physics or history just meant you'd been listening to the teacher, but to be good at English – the language we all have to speak anyway – was like being 'good at being a person', or 'excellent at living'. Now it's going to be called Understanding English, Communication and Languages, which is, like, sooooo lame, you know what I'm saying? I mean, bruv, who wants to communicate, innit?

A huge change of personality will come over the curriculum: the muscular thickos who can climb a rope but barely read will now shine in Understanding Physical Health and WellBeing, which sounds every bit the intellectual equal of Scientific and Technological Understanding. And all the subjects for whacked-out druggies with dirty hair will be lumped together as Understanding Arts and Design – although many will no doubt be put off by its having four words, which is way more than they are capable of reading at a sitting.

Nor is the death of 'subjects' the only great news. I was delighted to read that the new proposals will also 'offer summer-born children the chance to start school earlier so as not to miss out on vital months of education which can disadvantage them later in life'.

And thank the Lord for it. I was born on 29 July 1969, and as a result missed almost everything, especially Anglo-Saxon shore forts. Don't ask me why, but when I arrived in form 5G in September 1978 everyone already knew about them. I was desperate to be filled in, but we were on to 1066 now, and that was it. To admit to not knowing about Anglo-Saxon shore forts would have been academic death.

But, by sod's law, in almost every class discussion of the Conqueror's invasion that term (and even, tangentially, in discussion of Tostig's incursion via the Humber and the Ouse), the key seemed to be Anglo-Saxon shore forts, of which my fellow pupils had not only drawn innumerable pictures, but which they had apparently visited on more than one history field trip, while I was down the hall in 4W, excelling precociously in potato painting and looking up rude words in the dictionary (oh, the laughs I got with 'gaseous aftermath of an anal dilation').

But of Anglo-Saxon shore forts I knew nothing. The pain of ignorance was horrendous and to this very day, when asked any especially difficult question (such as, what speed I thought I was driving at, which wine I would like with the turbot, and whether it's worth taking the M25 round to the M20 or best just sticking with the A2), my first instinct is to assume that the answer has something to do with Anglo-Saxon shore forts.

The problem for me was that, as a summer child, I was always either the youngest or the oldest in the class. I began my school career, at five, as the youngest: endlessly failing, and cocking about in lessons to make up for it. So they wrote me off as 'puerile' (harsh criticism to the ears of a five-year-old who didn't know he was not supposed to be a '*puer*' any more) and dropped me down a year, where I became, of course, the oldest in the class, and took the job very seriously, coming top in everything and having – by the meritocratic system then in place in our schools – to be promoted the following year to the smarter, older class, where, obviously, it was a shock no longer to be top, and where I resorted to compensatory arsing about once more, leading to relegation, and so on.

Essentially a normal child with abilities bang on average in a decent school, my unlucky birth date meant that I was cast anew, each year, as either a dunce or a genius (each categorisation as erroneous as the other), which had exactly the effect on my impressionable mind that you might expect: I was the destructive swot, the naughty prizewinner, the thicko with the English cup. Never in one class long enough to make friends, never quite sure if this new crowd was behind or ahead of me.

At 15, I got the best O levels of anyone in the slow stream (which were worse than anyone in the fast stream) and so applied to Oxford, which took me at 16 but insisted I took a year out to 'grow up a bit'. So after school I went to work in Harrods as an elf in Santa's grotto. Just the thing.

And Sir Jim is right, one never quite catches up. To this very day, I consider myself a 40-year-old of pretty normal brightness and wit. Put me among 40-year-olds and I will shine like a beacon, but put me with 41-year-olds and I start pulling silly faces and weeing in corners.

The Death of Woolworths

The death of Woolworths has dealt a serious blow to those of us who had been quietly celebrating the onset of recession as a counterbalance to the recent years of greed and slickness, and had hoped that it would herald the arrival of a new austerity.

Secretly, I had been longing for a return to the stiff, cold, clip-voiced, monochromatic world of the early 1950s, or the Blitz, or the Great Depression, or the three-day week section of the 1970s, or, indeed, any of the impoverished and perilous periods of our recent past, which by rights ought to have been depressing, relentless and smelly, but about which old people bang on endlessly with a tear in the eye, remembering mostly the songs and the shagging.

I was all set to crack out a pair of horn-rimmed spectacles and a flat cap, grow a pencil moustache and belt my trousers around my armpits. I was looking forward to rubbish piled high in the streets, shoeless children in grey shorts playing cricket with shards of Spitfire in bombed-out cathedrals, family gatherings round the radio to hear optimistic prognostications from the Prime Minister (delivered from his nuclear bunker 10,000 ft beneath the Peak District), three-mile walks to get the milk, scratchy woollen Home Guard fatigues, boiled horsemeat and other things that could, in later years, be funnelled willy-nilly into sentences beginning: 'When I were a lad . . .'

And central to that delirious fantasy would have been shopping at Woolworths. When the money finally ran out, when the petrol pumps were empty and the bins overflowing, nothing in the larder but a Fray Bentos steak and kidney pie (19 years past its sell-by) and two dented tins of peas, then the only way to fully accept my fate would have been to slip on my Mister Byrite tank top and sturdy old Freeman Hardy Willises and head down to Woolworths to steal a pocketful of damp, botulism-flavoured marshmallows from the Pick'n'Mix, and then browse the cassette singles and Betamaxes (including *Rentaghost*, the Complete Second Series – only one tape missing), broken crockery, small pink Spice Girls tricycles (chained for security to the plastic dustbins you can get free from the council anyway), and maybe leave with K-Tel's *Favourite Number Twos of the 70s*, performed by the Brotherhood of Man, and a shaving mirror from which the price sticker, mounted slap in the middle, just about where your nose usually is, will never, ever, quite come off.

Because to have filled my house with stuff from Woolworths would have been to embrace properly the deflated spirit of the age. It is the place where you can get absolutely everything, but in its crappest form. The same stuff as everywhere else, only worse.

If you didn't want to spend 40 quid on fairy lights for the Christmas tree, you could spend £4 on fairy lights from Woolies. They wouldn't actually light up, of course, and when you gave one of the bulbs a tweak to check it was screwed in properly you'd get all your teeth blown out of your head and your hair set on fire. You might spend the rest of Christmas in A&E, but the main thing was you were only down £4.

And if £9 seemed too much for a glass pie dish from John Lewis then you could get one from Woolies for £2.50 that would be smashed into a thousand pieces by the time you got it home on the bus (Woolworths customers always go home on the bus). And if it wasn't, then it would shatter as soon as you turned on the oven.

Woolworths was for people who had no money but still wanted to buy things: 'Only £3 for this lidless thermos flask?' 'A mere fiver for this AM-only radio with a battery flap that doesn't quite close?' Best of all, it was sold to you by a surly woman wearing a badly pilled, red polyester fleece who suspected you of shoplifting. Oh, the wonder of it.

I love the crapola Britain signified by Woolies, and was so hoping that we would be driven back to it. I thought in these hard times it would be all the new shops and services that would go – all the fancy foreign imports, the good coffee, the colourful food, the sexy clothes, the slick technology – and that Britain would return to those days of long and seemingly endless yore when all things British were rubbish, and we just didn't care.

We had the worst food in the world, the dowdiest women, the dreariest men, the clumpiest footballers, the slowest cars, the laziest miners, the weediest fascists, the itchiest clothes, the smelliest drains, the thickest smog, the most depressing poetry, the angriest plays, no novelists at all and funny little moustachioed prime ministers who shot grouse and didn't know what a television was.

But the closure of Woolies suggests that the traditional core values of what I fondly call 'Crap Britain' are going to be lost, after all. The psoriatic, whooping baby is being thrown out with the fancily scented bathwater. Look at Little Chef, made over all poncy by Heston Fancy-Pants Blumenthal. It's all free-range eggs, green-tea trifle and 72-hour braised ox cheeks now.

And there was I, looking forward to embracing the grimness of the current climate by pulling off a wet dual carriageway to sit at a greasy table, swallowing slices of clumsily slaughtered factory pig washed down with bog-water coffee, then getting raped by a trucker in the outside loo.

Woolies, Little Chef, what next? Ginsters? Panda Pops? Mr

Whippy? It's all going. Almost all gone. The grey, damp, crappy underbelly of the ancient British consumer culture is being stripped away, and when this crash reaches its lowest point, who knows now what we will find there?

The March of Low Culture

I don't want to give you the wrong impression – and make you think that I give a gibbon's blue goolies whether or not John Sergeant and some horse-thighed Croatian belly-dancer were robbed of a chance to win *Strictly Come Dancing* by Sergeant's withdrawal from the competition under pressure from 'serious dance fans', but there was one vein of comment in the quagmire of cack spouted about it all that did, briefly, engage me.

And that came when the pro-Sergeant 'lobby' appeared to marshal itself around the rallying cry that 'the judges should lighten up, it's just a bit of fun, we need distracting from the grimness of the recession'. And I just absolutely do not agree. I cannot see the link. I do not grasp why global economic meltdown should necessarily create an appetite for dumb vanity and shallowness.

Dancing is a moronic activity at the best of times, and when turned into yet another opportunity for celebrity exhibitionism and flawed voting schemes that give democracy a bad name (among a viewing public too lazy to turn out in any significant numbers for elections that really might make a difference to their lives), it appears more imbecilic still. Fiddling while Rome burns. Whistling Dixie.

If a man has lost his job, if his children have holes in their shoes and he is living off soup made from the ninth boiling of a squirrel, then how dare we imagine that his lot will be eased by the sight of a retired journalist waddling round a dance floor with some thunder-bummed Siberian flosspot (or Slovenian or Russian or whatever she is – I've not seen the show but I've seen the photos in the paper, and nobody colours their hair and body like that except to compensate for a childhood lived under communism)?

The media, perhaps understandably, have turned very monochromatic of late. They have only two notes: mad, screaming pessimism about money on the one hand, and brutish, wailing enthusiasm for the lowest of low culture on the other. As if a lack of perspective at both ends in some way created balance.

This week, for example, the papers, when briefly turning their attention away from *Strictly Come Dancing*, have been thoroughly boob-struck, wrapping stories about the 'moral failure' of banks around photographs of Nigella with her shmams out, and running front-page headlines about families losing their homes alongside *I'm a Celebrity . . .* video-grabs of big, wet, plastic norks in the jungle.

I do not want to appear hypocritical here, for I am as easily distracted by a big artificial rack on a dim-witted WAG as the next man, but it's not a 'new Jordan' that this country should be looking for just at this precise moment, it's a new outlook on life. A far more serious and grown-up one.

And don't look up from your copy of the No. 1 bestseller *Look Who It Is! – My Story* by Alan Carr and give me 'escapism'. Escapism is an illusion. Escapism is what has got us into this mess. Buying on credit, from the tiddliest MasterCard lunch you couldn't really afford to billion-dollar leveraged buyouts, is, when you boil it down, just escapism – avoiding any sort of engagement with objective reality and doing something just because it feels good at the time. Like a child might do. Or a monkey.

This is not the time to waste a week of your life with Alan Carr's autobiography (or Dawn French's or Paul O'Grady's or Richard Madeley's) and think it counts as reading a book. Because it doesn't. You have borrowed unwisely. You have taken a week off your life that you will not get back at the end, and when you shut whichever compendium of venal drivel you chose, you will still owe thousands on your worthless home and be in no less danger of losing your job.

If you had at least read a bit of Tolstoy, you might have expanded your mind a little. If, instead of watching all those reality shows, you had learnt Japanese, you would be in a better position to remain in work. And if, rather than calling radio phone-ins to say that Len Goodman is a spoilsport, you had learnt the French horn, you would, if nothing else, be able to play your children a bit of Mozart while they sit shivering round the last candle in the house.

I cannot tell you how furious I am with these people who seem to think they should be given back the money they spent on voting for John Sergeant. Anyone to whom a single pound represents a significant, useful quantity of money, and who spent it on a celebrity game show vote, should have his or her assets frozen immediately – under the counter-terrorism laws if need be. Their children should be taken into care. And they should have their credit cards melted and moulded into a stick with which they should be flogged until they bleed.

How in the world can people be angry about a game show? How can a country in 2008 (with the National Intelligence Council in America predicting 20 impending years of environmental tragedy and nuclear war) truly divide into two camps on the question of whether or not the dancing, per se, is the lifeblood of *Strictly Come Dancing*? It's not funny. It's not even wholesome. It is rancid. If the people who have got so angry about the 'injustice' of John's departure had any balls, they would be out lynching bankers.

The point is that all these distractions and escape channels were created not by recession but, quite the opposite, by economic boom.

It was the fat years that made us lazy, dumbed us down, replaced great television with a series of reality shows and killed literature to make room for celebrity whingeing and kiddy books repackaged for adults. It is no coincidence that the publication cycle of *Harry Potter*, from the first book to the seventh, marked almost exactly the years of economic growth. It is a fat, lazy race that turns its brain off as a prelude to cultural engagement.

Fat, like the seven fat kine in Pharaoh's dream, and the seven lean kine that came after and ate them up. We laid nothing by in the fat years except shlock and dross, and now we turn to it and find that it offers us nothing. Shopping as leisure activity, for heaven's sake. Bluewater, Lakeside, Westfield. The descent into Gomorrah is all-encompassing and headlong. We have not just lost our money, we have lost everything.

Sensible investment designed to repay over the long term would not have screwed everything up the way wild speculation for short-term profit has done.

And the same is true in the culture. Things are going to be pretty crappy now for quite some time, and the short-term fixes of reality television and celebrity biography are not going to help.

It would be a great thing if bad times meant we found room for proper books again, and slightly less poisonous popular culture. In the long run, we will end up feeling better if we moderate the gloom of a life with less money by focusing on higher things, not lower ones.

The US Open

I am here today to save tennis (or, rather, to save Wimbledon, which is what we Englishmen mean when we say 'tennis') because, thanks to Andy Murray, I found myself watching the US Open this year for the first time in my life and: Oh. My. God.

The court was blue! And when they bounced the ball before serving it made this horrible 'pock, pock, pock' noise like a postman knocking on the door of a Portakabin. That was when you could hear anything at all, what with the courts apparently having been built in the car park at JFK, so that there was rarely more than a minute's peace between the passing overhead of each aeroplane. I SAID: 'RARELY MORE THAN A MINUTE's . . .'

And the clothes, ye gods. Freed from the Wimbledon dress code, Murray wore the black trainers of an urban mugger and an old T-shirt the colour of a Possil towerblock. And I don't know what in the world Federer thought he had come as, with his brown shorts and red blouse. He looked like Minnie Mouse.

The line judges, in their blue jogging pants and comfy white trainers, looked like elderly Floridians dressed for a power walk around the buffet table. And the umpire wore a baseball cap and a bomber jacket, sitting there watching the kids play tennis like a suburban paedophile. No wonder the crowd (spread out like collapsing soufflés in their giant seats) whistled and hooted through the rallies – no authority. No sense of occasion.

The ball boys were incongruously tall, tanned and chunky – they must feed them well at Barnardo's over there. And they threw the balls overarm. Where's the respect?

The changeovers were ten minutes long to make room for

commercials, so that the players spent more time sitting down than they did playing, and the courtside was covered in bank logos. Then, when it was over, all they talked about was money.

They asked Federer how it felt to win $1.5 million, like he was some slack-jawed lottery punter who got lucky. Like it was polite to talk about money in public. And then they handed him the keys to his free Lexus right there on court. I tried to imagine the Duchess of Kent doing something similar, perhaps sprawled across the bonnet in a bikini.

Who knows, maybe the free executive saloon with its capacious boot was the most exciting thing for Federer. Now that he won't have to schlep his kit around on the bus any more, who knows how far he can go in the game?

Every year they push the boundaries in SW19: a flash of colour here, a logo there. But I have seen the ghost of Wimbledon future. And it must be prevented.

Motorbikes

I gather that the electric motorcycle, already very popular in India, is to be introduced into Britain. This is a challenging proposition for me, because I hate motorbikes more than anything. Anything. More than Nazis, bungee-jumpers and dog poo all rolled into one (ooh, yuk).

I hate them for the noise that they make, and how their riders just don't care that their journey from A to B briefly ruins the lives of countless thousands along their route.

I hate the teenagers on my block who race their screeching scooters up and down the street all day, their helmets sitting back high on their heads so that they are looking out from under them, doing wheelies in their skanky grey sweatpants and prison-white trainers, killing time until dusk, when the crack barons start chucking them courier work.

I hate motorbikes because they fill the gaps in waves of urban traffic, so that just when you think it's safe to pull out, some arsehole appears from nowhere doing 140 mph, so that you ram on your brakes to save his life, and he flips you a rigid middle finger for your efforts.

And I hate them for rocketing up between lanes on busy high streets (illegally overtaking stationary traffic) and killing people who are just trying to cross the road.

I hate the ones who deliver obesity in big flat boxes of starch and processed cheese, about whom I have said enough in the past, God rot them.

And most of all I hate the mopeds ridden by traffic wardens, who are theoretically employed to keep traffic moving and streets safe, but in fact create an extra circuit of slow-moving traffic around the pavement, double-parking to squint into windscreens, clipping wing mirrors, gratuitously polluting the atmosphere because they are too lazy or too greedy to walk (and, at the same time, depriving communities of the single, tiny benefit that they once provided, of representing a pair of uniformed eyes and ears in the absence of beat policemen).

The great thing about the electric motorbike is that it doesn't make any noise, so it won't wake anyone up, it doesn't smell and it doesn't go very fast so won't screw up the traffic flow, and thus will also be of no use for teeny crack-deal getaways, which means that, er, oh, I guess nobody will buy one.

XFM Drivetime

I was listening to XFM's Drivetime show the other day when I heard something that made me very angry indeed. So angry, that I don't think I can bear to express that anger. I think it might kill me.

So I'm just going to tell you what I heard, and not say what I think about it. I'm just going to repeat it, and then you can think whatever you like.

The DJ, I forget his name, was broadcasting live from Ibiza (*Eye-beeffa*) and had decided to play a game where he phoned up local record shops to ask if they had certain albums by bands that (hilariously) don't actually exist. The hilarity would apparently ensue from the local (obviously Spanish) staff not knowing what he was talking about, but trying their best to be helpful.

The British in Spain, it makes you so proud.

So anyway, he phoned a shop and the guy was awfully nice, and each time this DJ said: ''Ave you got ennyfink by Chubby-Chasing Tree Surgeons on Gack' (or whatever), the nice record shop guy said: 'No, sorry, I am not have zees', and the morons in the studio fell about.

And then the DJ said: 'Last fing, mate, 'ave you got "The Diarrhoea of Anne Frank"?'

That would be Anne Frank, the little Dutch girl whose 'diary' (you see what they did there?) of her years in hiding from the Nazis ended abruptly when she was captured, taken to Belsen and died there from typhus, contracted because of the terrible sanitary conditions (no sewerage, you see, just buckets of diarrhoea in the corner).

Ha ha.

Ha ha ha ha ha.

Poland

Lügner

On Tuesday we buried my great-uncle Gus. Most of the service was in Hebrew and I spent it, as I always do at these occasions, glancing at the prayerbooks of the men around me, trying to guess, from the shapes of the separate masses of indecipherable script in their hands, which page I was supposed to be on.

Fortunately, the bit about what a kind, successful and funny chap Gus was (which he absolutely was – he was a Coren, after all) was in English, and I was able to liven up and pay attention. And then the rabbi started talking about 'Gus's father, Harry, who came here from central Poland as a teenager . . .'

I remember my great-grandpa Harry very well. The patriarch. The first Coren. I am the only son of the only son of his first son, and I have always considered that, in my solipsistic way, to be a very big deal.

I remember his 90th birthday party in 1975, sitting on his knee, kissing his face and feeling the coarse whiskers against my lips. I remember being pleased that he was exactly the same age as my favourite football team, QPR, which was founded in 1885.

Thirty-three years later, standing at the funeral of his last surviving son, the women on one side, men on the other, Gus in a box in front of us with a cloth over it bearing the Star of David, I thought how interesting it was, at a time when many of the current generation of Polish immigrants are said to be returning home because the construction work is drying up, that we were all still here – dozens of us descended from a single Pole who came in 1903 – more than 100 years later. Not one of us has gone back. Even to visit.

That is the difference between the two kinds of migration, you see. The economic and the humanitarian. We Corens are here, now, because the ancestors of these Poles now going home used to amuse themselves at Easter by locking Jews in the synagogue and setting fire to it. Harry didn't leave in the hope of finding a better life. Just a life. The option to return was not there for him, for obvious reasons, and by 1945 the Poland he had left did not exist any more. My sympathy for the plight of the modern Pole is thus limited, and if England is not the land of milk and honey it appeared to them three or four years ago, then, frankly, they can clear off out of it.

When I got home from the funeral I read about the capture of Radovan Karadžić, and saw footage of some of the genocide that he himself instigated so recently, so near to Poland. Serbia has hunted him down, it is said, because it wants to join the EU. But the European Union is not so fussy as it once was. Virulently racist populist politicians hold significant power now in Central and Eastern Europe, and the modern, expand-at-all-costs EU is not bothered by that at all.

Only this week, a Radio 4 programme revealed plans by the Lithuanian state prosecutor (with the full support of Lithuania's Deputy Foreign Minister, Jaroslavas Neverovicas) to charge former members of the Jewish resistance in Lithuania – escapees from the ghetto, who were fighting for their lives – with war crimes. As state-sponsored anti-Semitism, it makes Jörg Haider (remember him?), with his mild nostalgia for shiny leather boots and concentration camps, seem terribly innocuous.

Lithuania – which was part of the same state as Poland until 1795 and, like Poland, but unlike Germany, has never gone through any process of recrimination for, or even fully acknowledged, its role in the Holocaust – had an impressive war record, wiping out 95 per cent of its Jewish population, 200,000 people, with very little help from the invaders.

Since then it has shown no interest in prosecuting its own war criminals. And now it's decided that it was all the Jews' fault – again. Don't expect Poland not to follow suit.

Following the publication of this piece, the Poles went postal. Literally and metaphorically. *The Times* was bombarded with letters from Poles all over the world, outraged that I had accused them of being in denial about their responsibility for the Holocaust. And strongly denying any responsibility for the Holocaust.

I particularly enjoyed one from Barbara Tuge-Erecińska, the Ambassador of the Republic of Poland to the United Kingdom, in which she stated that: 'Poland's role in the tragedy of the Holocaust consists in the fact that the extermination of the Jewish people happened to take place on Polish territory.' To which one can only say 'Ha bloody ha di ha ha ha' and fall on the floor laughing. And slightly vomiting.

I invited her, in print, to write again and this time tell us about the Kielce pogrom of 1946, 15 months after the war finished. Most of my readers, I said, didn't know about the widespread killing, by Poles, only by Poles, not by anyone else, of Polish Jews returning from the camps after their liberation. But she declined to do so.

On and on they ranted, defacing my Wikipedia site (much as their ancestors once desecrated the synagogues of Warsaw before the arrival of the Nazis gave them the excuse they needed to start killing the worshippers themselves) with all sorts of crazed, self-deluding bollocks about how they never done nuffink, guv, it was all them Germans.

Indeed, many of them were at pains to tell me how the majority of those named by Israel as 'Righteous Gentiles' were Polish and only one or two British. To which one has to say, 'That, chum, is because there was no slaughter of Jews going on in Britain to stand up against. In Poland, there was SOMETHING TO

BE RIGHTEOUS ABOUT!!' A few hundred decent men and women, out of the millions, standing up for their neighbours is hardly something to get excited about.

Sure, the Poles were victims of the Nazis, and that is its own tragedy, and I acknowledge and lament it. But the ludicrous evasions and refusals of modern Poles to accept the sins of their fathers is a grotesque blot on their national character.

The case was referred to the Press Complaints Commission by the Federation of Poles in Great Britain (which my Wikipedia defacers brag about) but was thrown out (which they do not – indeed, whenever I try to add that fall-out to the case history online, it is removed).

In preparing my defence to the PCC, I was specifically asked to defend the statement that the Poles 'used to amuse themselves at Easter by locking Jews in the synagogue and setting fire to it'. And I have to admit that finding evidence for the statement was difficult. The Poles did an awful lot of rounding up of Jews into town halls and barns and then burning them alive (as, for example, at Jedwabne in July 1941 – described in the chilling *Neighbors* by Jan T. Gross, Princeton, 2001); and they did a lot of burning of synagogues which killed only one or two, as well as a lot of pogroms at Easter in which Jews were killed in the street. But an actual instance of a mass rounding up in a synagogue and then setting light to it and killing everyone inside was harder to find.

You can imagine, no doubt, how delightful the days were as I was forced to trawl through endless accounts of gruesome Polish massacres of innocent Jewish civilians, looking for the 'right' one. Truly there were moments I punched the air and shouted 'Yes!' as I read 'The Jews were rounded up into the synagogue and burned alive' and then cried 'Fuck!' as I discovered that it had happened in August, not at Easter.

For a time it looked as if I was going to have to issue an apology along the lines of, 'I am so sorry to have suggested that the Poles used to round up Jews at Easter and burn them alive in the synagogue. It turns out the Poles are not that awful after all. They actually did it mostly in barns.' But then I found the evidence I needed, and that was that.

My Wikipedia Poles claim that the case is currently being looked at by the European Court of Human Rights. But I very much doubt that.

They also claim that when asked for a comment by the *Jewish Chronicle*, I replied, by email, 'Fuck the Poles'.

So I suppose that must be true.

The Attempt to Democratise Oxbridge Entrance

The best thing about A level season is the teenage girls in summer dresses tossing their blonde hair and giggling over fake envelopes on the front of *The Daily Telegraph*. The worst thing is the annual guff about inequality in the university entrance systems.

'The spread of individual university entrance exams, the arrival of the A*, and the proliferation of new qualifications . . .' *The Guardian* claimed last time, 'could make this a very uneven playing field.'

In short, everyone now gets straight As and universities are having to find other ways of discriminating between identical candidates. These methods are (inevitably) class-biased, and once again there won't be very many poor people going to Oxford or Cambridge.

Boring. Borrrrrrrrring. Boring, boring, boring. I am so fed up with being made to feel guilty for getting into Oxford only because I went to a school that gave me a posh voice, fluent conversational Latin, three top hats and a brief friendship with the eldest son of the Earl of Sandwich. Even if it's true. I'm just boooooooored with it.

So I've come up with a solution: ban public schoolboys from going to university altogether.

The truth is that if you go to a half-decent private school you arrive at university knowing as much as you're going to need to pass a modern university exam anyway (only this week, staff at Manchester Metropolitan University were told to start ramping up exam marks to bring the place up to the national average of providing firsts and upper seconds for fully 60 per cent of candidates).

As a result, public school kids spend at least two years waiting for the 'less fortunate' kids to get up to where they were at 15. Far better to get out into the workplace and start earning money than to borrow it from the government so you can spend three years getting drunk and going to parties, smoking dope and falling out of windows until, at the end of it all, you are as thick as everyone else.

This will be good for the underprivileged students, too. Because it is not much fun for them arriving at college in their flat caps, smelling of stale beer and roll-ups, and finding themselves outclassed by a lot of pink-faced twonks in straw boaters. That's why they so often go into their shells and end up wearing black and listening to The Fall and not looking people in the eye. If the posh kids weren't there, they would be able to shine.

It's not like the banned public schoolboys would be missing out on anything worthwhile. After all, if you have been at an OK public school then you've already had at least five years of living in grand old buildings with good libraries, being taught by teachers who respect your opinions. How much more of that do you need?

If you have too much, you end up like Boris Johnson or David Cameron, having to get fat and pretend to be stupid just so people won't be afraid of you.

University can make a bright young mind complacent. Get a top-class degree from Oxford or Cambridge (by falling off a log) and you feel you have nothing left to prove.

But look at chaps like A.A. Gill and Jonathan Meades, two of our cleverest writers, neither of whom went to university but learnt all the clever stuff they know by themselves. As a result, they try much harder to get that clever stuff into their writing, which contributes to our huge reading pleasure.

A chap who proved all that stuff years ago doesn't really bother, and just churns out any old guff, I'd imagine.

For universities merely to look a bit more favourably on state school kids where possible is not enough. It will never effect the social revolution that we all crave. We must take a sledgehammer to crack this particular social nut.

The modern university, a place for drinking and shagging and getting a top-class degree as a reward for remembering to wear clothes to the exams, is a waste of time if you have been educated properly already.

Far better to get out early with your 37 As and go straight into a job, where you can set about feathering your nest, employing your buddies and making sure there are no jobs left for the oiks when they finally come down from Oxford.

J.K. Rowling

It just isn't going to end, it isn't ever going to end. There are going to be new *Harry Potter* books coming out every year for the rest of my life. I just know it.

That blasted woman promised she was only going to write seven of them and then stop. But she lied. She just rotten lied, purely to push up the value of the ones she has published already. It's like the diamond market. She is the De Beers of literature, hoarding away tons of this intrinsically worthless stock, for which people have an inexplicable and very base lust, and trickling it out on to the market gradually, for billions, under the threat of an impending (and imaginary) shortfall in supply.

And as the price of *Potter* goes up, so the size of the books comes down (which is, at least, a blessing). First there was *The Tales of Beedle the Bard*, only 157 pages and with a print run cunningly restricted to seven books, of which only one came on to the market and was sold to Amazon (see that? sold *to* Amazon, not *by* Amazon) for £1.95 million. That's good business, that is.

After that, Rowling clearly decided to see how far she could push the maths, and has now produced a book of only 800 words, written 'in minuscule handwriting' on a single piece of A5.

Eight hundred words! Rowling has grasped that, with her stock this high, 800 is about as many words as she needs to write. If she has anything in common with her fellow writers (and she doesn't have much) it is clearly laziness. There is not a novelist alive who would not stop writing after 800 words, if he thought he could get away with it.

The book has been produced for a charity auction (I am not

for a minute suggesting that Rowling is avaricious, just smart) and is apparently some sort of a prequel. Ooh, how exciting. It's Harry Potter before he could do magic. What is it, a Jennings book?

But, come on, 800 words. Where will it end? The original *Harry Potter* books kept getting longer and longer (the crackhead lit-kids who came out annually to score them at midnight needing bigger and bigger doses to 'feel something'), and now she is going the other way.

Will her next great oeuvre contain 400 words? 200? 83?

Laurence Sterne risked a single blank page in Tristram Shandy (as well as one black one). Georges Perec made a bold stab at a full-length novel with no 'e's in it (and Gilbert Adair made an even bolder stab at translating it – lipogram intact – from French into English). B.S. Johnson put a lot of loose pages in a box and said it was finished. But the great pranksters and innovators of the past will have to hold up their hands and admit defeat if Rowling truly makes a go of the one-page novel.

And what of all the great novelists who never got around to banging out prequels to their greatest works, for fear that they didn't have much to say about events before the narrative began, or thought they didn't have enough time for such a craven endeavour?

Little did Charles Dickens dream that there might be two million quid in a bit of paper that said: 'Congratulations, Mrs Twist – it's a boy!'

And perhaps Herman Melville would not have lived such a life of penury if he had had the nous to publish a prequel to his most famous work featuring a single scene, in which a couple walk into a Nantucket bookshop, the wife clearly eight and a half months pregnant, pick up a book of baby names and open it randomly at the letter 'I'.

Hell, if they'd followed the Rowling model the blokes who

wrote the Book of Genesis could have scratched 'It was a dark and stormy night' on to a scrap of papyrus and moved to California.

And who is to say it will end here? Who knows how far Rowling can take this? How short can she go?

Whenever I am asked, 'Have you read the new *Harry Potter*?', I reply, for form's sake, 'I'm halfway through but not really getting into it, I'm afraid'. The next time I try that one, will my inquisitor protest, 'But it's only two words long'?

No doubt, as her final great gift to literacy in English, Rowling will eventually produce a novel that comprises a single piece of paper – valued at £90 million – on which is written simply the word: 'Wizard'.

And no doubt, as some wealthy but barely literate teenager pores over it for endless hours in her suburban bedroom, her parents will say defensively: 'Well, at least it's got her reading . . .'

Cycling Helmets

At the memorial service for my old English teacher, Jim Cogan, a great scholar and adventurer, a fearless sailor, a defiant burrower into the dark heart of Africa, and a man who never, ever wore a cycling helmet, his friend James Flecker recalled Jim's nighttime cycle journeys through London without lights, without helmet, suit trousers tucked into socks, a wobbling road phantom unmoved by intimations of mortality.

And he told how one morning, arriving at an office they shared together, he, Flecker, took off his cycling helmet and laid it on his desk. Then put down his flashing red and white lights. Then took off his high-visibility vest and was just removing the second of his luminous trouser clips when Jim, who had been watching this awesome display of road sense, sighed and said: 'For the Lord's sake, James, at least die like a man.'

I thought of Jim the other day when I saw Boris Johnson apologising for cycling without a helmet, and promising to wear one in future. And I thought: 'You big sissy, Boris. You frilly bloody great girl. You've gone and blown it.'

And he has, you know. He has let his guard down under the pressure of office, and shown that he is as much a slave to the vain, modern quest for immortality as any vegan actress or eco-crazed old pop star. And is thus, now, utterly pointless.

I had thought Boris was one of us. I thought he grasped that eternal truth that to be unafraid of life, you must first be unafraid of death.

One of the great reasons for respecting Boris, despite everything, was his devil-may-care attitude to cycling. And, indeed, to everything. There are a lot of crap and embarrassing things about being an old-fashioned English toff, but fearing desperately for one's life has never been one of them.

Boris looks silly, sounds silly, says silly things, and went to a silly school, but what he offered, we thought, was a sort of old-fashioned bluffness in the face of peril, the stoicism and wit of an Empire builder who would demonstrate, in these post-Imperial days, that there are other things that such a man can build.

I used to look at Boris and think of Henry Newbolt:

> *The river of death has brimmed its banks,*
> *And England's far, and Honour a name,*
> *But the voice of a schoolboy rallies the ranks –*
> *'Play up! Play up! And play the game!'*

But you can't play the game in a polyurethane bonce-protector, Boris. That's not how it works. (Indeed the very sport from which Newbolt draws his analogy, cricket, ceased to be a game for gentlemen at the very moment that batsmen began wearing helmets – why should I pause in my busy life to watch the antics of men so femininely fearful of personal injury?)

The cycle helmet is one of the great emblems of the failure of 21st-century manhood, like the seatbelt, and the gymnasium, and the low-fat diet, and the airbag, and the sunblock, and the one-aspirin-a-day.

It's just so vulgar to treasure one's mortal coil this brazenly. To wear so publicly one's trembling, pasty-faced fear of death.

You mustn't care if you die, Boris. Fear of death is for Them, not Us. To worry overmuch about the extinction of any human is a post-Enlightenment vanity. There is no shortage of people. Least of all of people like you and me – silly men, born to privilege, succeeding beyond all expectation on the back of a self-confidence to which we are scarcely entitled and opportunities we have not earned – no shortage of daft buggers to step in and take your place if you crack your head on a lamppost.

Road safety is a mirage, anyway. I have never worn a cycling helmet and I never will. For it creates a false sense of security, not to mention making you look too unsexy to whistle at girls.

For the same reasons, I have never worn a seatbelt in a car (and have the copious licence endorsements to prove it). It's scratchy and annoying and pulls at your clothes. It creates a sense of cockpit security that encourages me to drive faster. And also it creases my shirt, which is a waste of ironing.

I am very much with the chap from RoSPA who said that the surest way to ensure road safety would be to mount a six-inch spike in the middle of every steering wheel.

Get your helmet off, Boris. They voted for you because you don't wear it. That's your whole thing. Don't listen to the wet-eyed mummies at the school gates or the Trots in the mayoral press office. Get it off. Play the game. And if there's a bump out there with your name on it, then, for the Lord's sake, Boris, at least die like a man.

Adverts

The Broadcast Committee of Advertising Practice (BCAP) has, at long last, ruled that television adverts can no longer be louder than the programmes in which they appear.

Better late than never, I suppose. I have mostly given up watching television because of the shrieking of the adverts. It's just so horrible how you're sitting there on the sofa after dinner, vaguely watching some costume drama with ladies in bonnets on a river bank sharing out the egg sandwiches, and trout taking the fly with a muted 'glop', and you're half asleep and drifting into a sort of reverie where you're asking Miss Bennet if there isn't, perchance, a slice of cucumber to be had hereabouts, and she raises her long eyelashes and says:

'BUY STUFF! BUY STUFF NOW!! RA RA RA!! BLAAAAA!! KRANG!!!! BUY LOADS OF IT!!!! ONLY NINE NINE NINE FIVE!! COME DOWN TO THE CRAPHOLE WAREHOUSE!! SOFAS CAN GO UP AS WELL AS DOWN MAY CAUSE HEATBURN IN PREGNANT BABIES!!'

And you leap up thinking hoodies are at the door and grab your tennis racket and run out naked into the street. And then you realise it was just the ads.

I guess it is because television is so dismal that the ads are so loud. The advertisers know that whoever sits down to watch *Britain's Got Property Ladders, Get Me Out of Here!* is bound to be asleep within minutes and if you want to tell them about the terrible disposable garbage you think they should buy with the money they don't have because they spend their whole pathetic life in front of the television, then first you're going to have to

WAKE THEM UP!! WAAAA!! BANG! BANG! BANG! DON'T SHOP FOR IT!!! ARGOS IT!!! WHATEVER THE HELL THAT MEANS!!! WA! WA!!! IT'S THE SAME OLD CRUD AS BEFORE, YOU JUST DON'T HAVE TO HAUL YOUR BIG GREEDY ARSE OFF THE SOFA TO GET IT!!

And if the viewers aren't asleep, then they've almost certainly gone into the kitchen to make a cup of tea and there is a chance that, from there, if the volume doesn't suddenly soar, they won't be able to hear some D-list celebrity saying: 'BUY FROZEN PEAS!!! THEY'RE GREAT!!! MUCH BETTER THAN FRESH!!!! SEALS IN THE FLAVOUR!!!! HURRAH FOR BIRDSEYE!! WAAA! WAAA!!!!'

But these new regulations state that 'adverts must not be excessively noisy or strident'. It's my dream come true. At half-time in the football, from now on, there will be a faint tinkle of theme music and then a chap in suede shoes and a V-neck will say, quite quietly: 'Why not have a Carlsberg, it's perfectly acceptable beer.'

And then there will be a car, sitting nice and still by the road, and a voice saying softly: 'Here's a car, it's much like all the others. If your own car is beyond repair, this is one of the many essentially identical vehicles you might consider as a replacement.' And so on.

And from this great start can we not go still further to reduce the depressing and deleterious aspects of advertising? Can we not, perhaps, make the abdominal muscles of those men in the aftershave ads a bit less ludicrous? Nobody has abs like that. And can we make them a bit less handsome? And those enormous bulges you see in the pants ads, I think it's time they were scaled down.

And those big perky breasts on the girls in the beer adverts – they're just not good for marriages. Come on, let's saggy them down a bit so the missus doesn't feel quite so critically scrutinised coming out of the shower.

In fact, let's do away with hyperbole altogether. No more *Ford Super Sunday* – just *Another Irrelevant Football Match Sponsored by a Mediocre Car Company Sunday*.

No more 'Fifty Greatest Comedy Moments' but 'Fifty Joyless Clips to Which We Already Had the Rights So It Cost Us Nowt'.

And once we're making some things a bit less noisy and strident, mightn't it be possible to make everything a bit less noisy and strident? Could they maybe turn the neon signs in Piccadilly Circus down a fraction? It would look so much classier. And might they be able to turn the volume down in the headphones of the guy sitting next to you on the Tube? And maybe also on the phones of the teenagers on the top deck of the bus because, really, this isn't a hip-hop gig, it's a frigging bus. And that courier roaring off to the next set of traffic lights, can't we turn the sound down on his motorbike? Or kill him?

And the fat blokes outside the pub with their shirts off, could we please turn off their tattoos? And must their trainers be quite so blindingly white? And whose idea was birdsong at dawn? And newspaper columnists these days, will they ever shut up?

McDonald's

The choice of Bruce Oldfield to redesign the staff uniforms at McDonald's seems to me the most futile exercise in turd-polishing since Adolf Hitler looked in the mirror and thought to himself: 'Hmm, maybe I'd look better with a little moustache.'

Ever since the world woke up to the obesity, heart disease, cancer, impotence and misery that a fast-food diet inevitably leads to, McDonald's has done everything in its power to deflect attention away from its hamburgers and on to other things.

They tried putting salads on the menu. But the salads turned out, it was said, to have more calories in them than the Big Macs. They tried a general overhaul of outlets in posher areas, dropping the red and yellow and going over to muted charcoal and pastels, hoping to encourage attractive young professionals to 'hang out' there, as if it were the Central Perk café in *Friends* ('The one in which Rachel balloons to 18 stone and Ross suffers a massive coronary'). But it didn't work.

And now this. They're still going to be selling the products that lie at the heart of Britain and America's very serious obesity crisis, not to mention the litter crisis, the deforestation crisis, the animal welfare crisis and the nasty smell up and down your high street crisis; but they're going to be doing it in black-and-white semi-fitted shirts and fluted skirts. So that's OK, then.

Bruce Oldfield himself even admitted that 'it was a big challenge to come up with something that would work for a huge range of sizes and shapes'.

Yup, that's Mickey D's for you: a huge range of sizes and shapes. Except that we're people, not flat-pack furniture. We're not meant to come in a huge range of sizes and shapes. We're meant to be the size and shape of people. Seems to me the solution to a 23-stone woman shaped like a potato is to get her out of McDonald's and on to a healthy diet. Not just create a giant, potato-shaped dress.

It's not as if the man who designed so many of Princess Diana's favourite dresses hasn't already done his bit to highlight the problems of a poor diet. Indeed, it looks like a pretty bold move from the inventors of the Filet-O-Fish and the McFlurry to call in a man so closely associated with celebrity barf.

But the fact is that some brands sometimes just get tarnished for ever, and since Morgan Spurlock's 2004 film *Super Size Me*, McDonald's has become one of those brands. Like Union Carbide, I.G. Farben, Nestlé, Ratners, Northern Rock, Thalidomide, Manchester City FC . . .

And, anyway, I don't think punters really want to be served by a better-dressed burger-flipper.

We usually go into McDonald's because we feel terrible. Drunk, hungry, hung-over, barely £2 in our pocket, all self-respect out the window, we push past the weeny bike thieves and kitten-stabbers gathered in the doorway. We keep our stomach together despite the slide of our feet on the cow-greased floor (is there ever not a sign up telling you the floor is slippery?) and the smell of a Swaledale field at the height of the cow-burning epidemic.

We catch sight of ourselves in those mirrors, lit by the merciless white neon overheads (I swear, I still have teenage acne in those mirrors), we jostle amid the giant-arsed women and the bag-snatchers who have come in only because KFC is shut and are grumbling about the high cost of the chicken nuggets, and when we finally come to order, we do not want to be made to talk, thank you very much indeed, to Helena bleeding Christensen.

You know what I mean? We want a spotty teenage loser in a skid-mark-coloured shirt that drains all the colour from his pasty face. We want a woman, squeezing between the chip-fryer and the milkshake machine, in a blouse you could make into outfits for a whole Brownie pack. We want a man whose polyester shirt sparks in the dark and out of which the smell of BO can never quite be washed. We want someone, in short, who is even lower down the food chain than we are. Someone in whose opinion we are not even slightly interested.

And in front of whom we will not feel bad about buying this crap (in much the same way, I simply cannot buy a porn mag from a beautiful female newsagent – a commodity that is in thankfully short supply). But if we are confronted by some elegant little thing in a designer dress, all clingy, tight little silhouette, curve of back and bulge of breast, then we are going to walk straight out again. We can't have her see us like this.

At the very least, we are going to change our order to a glass of orange juice and a salad. We are going to resolve, on the spot, to change our dietary ways to enable us to dream of scoring with somebody who is dressed by Bruce Oldfield.

The Best Job in the World

All the papers were saying that a man from Petersfield in Hampshire had just landed the 'best job in the world'. I was intrigued. Had this Ben Southall fellow been made director of the Sydney Opera? Had he been selected for the England cricket team? Had he been put in charge of a major company, newspaper or television station? Was he starting on Monday as our new prime minister? Would he be driving a steam train? Going to the Moon?

Don't be silly. This is 2009. We must recalibrate our ideas of what constitutes a dream job. We must dumb down our expectations a little. He had got a presenting role on *Top Gear*, had he? Or been made manager of Manchester United? No? What, then, surely he had not been put in charge of the thong laundry at the Playboy Mansion?

Again, no. The job that Ben had landed, ahead of thousands of applicants to a very public recruitment drive from Tourism Queensland, was a job as a caretaker.

Yes, sure, it was a caretaker job on an island off the Great Barrier Reef, so the weather would be nice and there'd be fish to eat. And the salary, at £75,000, was very respectable. But it was pretty mind-blowing to find the world's media heralding it as the best job in the world. No disrespect to caretakers, but their work is not usually considered especially rewarding. Nor is it undertaken, as a rule, by only the very best of the best.

Thinking back to my schooldays, and the genial, plodding brown-coats in milk-bottle spectacles, with their keys and their buckets and their little stepladders, I don't recall thinking that if only I knuckled down, read hard and stayed out of trouble, that could be me one day. The only significant caretaker, or janitor as they are called in America, that I can think of is Hong Kong Phooey. And he was famously useless and depended on a sarcastic cat to do all his crime-solving.

The job hunt was conceived mainly to raise awareness of Hamilton Island in the Whitsundays as a tourist destination, and the whittling down of 35,000 applicants proceeded very much along reality television lines, with Mr Southall reaching a final that involved 15 applicants from different countries. Although, since nobody apart from British people would ever dream of going on holiday to Australia, the other 14 needn't have bothered showing up. How many extra hotel beds would they have filled on Hamilton if the winner of the dream job had been Bangladeshi, say, or Malawian?

Ben impressed the judges, apparently, with a range of hobbies that included 'running, climbing, scuba diving, bungee jumping, mountain biking and organising music festivals'. So, clearly, the man is a moron. Or possibly a monkey. 'Ooh look,' one can imagine the chimpanzee personnel manager saying, 'this one is into running, jumping and climbing.'

On top of all that leaping about, Ben had to do a lot of blogging (another activity that requires no more skill or aptitude than you'd find in any weaned primate) and then iced the cake by handing out daffodils on Mother's Day, organising a cork-bobbing contest and swimming in the Thames. You want to guess how old he is? 12? 15? (Higher, higher.) 21? 27? Guess again, loser, the champion bungee-jumper and cork-bobber is a staggering 34-years-old. Thirty-frickin-four!

That makes him the same age as the all-but-retired David Beckham and only three years younger than George Osborne.

Thrilled at the prospect of the beachside villa that comes with the job, Mr Southall said that it would make a comfortable change because 'I stayed in a tent on top of my Land Rover last year while I travelled through Africa'.

Last year? What on earth was a man in early middle age doing travelling round Africa for a whole year? It's the gap-year mentality gone mad. Is nobody fit for anything but travel any more? Is aimlessly farting one's way around the world truly the summit of man's expectations?

I suppose it must be. Because it seems that what makes this caretaking job the best in the world is that it carries no responsibilities, duties or pressures. That it involves doing absolutely nothing at all.

The sort of people who will covet Mr Southall's job are those people one occasionally meets who dream of emigrating to Australia. 'For pity's sake, why?' you ask, agog.

'For the lifestyle,' they reply.

Ah yes, lifestyle. The great myth. The supreme Australian invention. 'Lifestyle' basically means that you can get drunk outdoors wearing only your pants all year round. And eat nothing but char-broiled food for the rest of your life. People who dream of emigrating there don't care what job they do, only that after it finishes each day they can go straight to the beach – where their only hope of avoiding skin cancer is to be eaten by a shark.

There is a Sunday morning 'nightclub' for Australians at the bottom of my road. It is called (with a brutal, blasphemous and typically Australian disregard for the culture of the host nation) 'the Church', and means that every Sunday the streets of Kentish Town are full of Aussies, in fancy dress with traffic cones on their heads, fighting and shouting and throwing up.

I just cannot understand how it could be considered an enviable thing to land a job that involves doing absolutely nothing all day in a land where the natives can't have fun without ending up in casualty dressed as a kangaroo.

Cheap Britain

One of Britain's most senior tourism chiefs (ooh, what an important man) has warned that bad service, grumpy staff and poor hygiene risk putting off foreign visitors, destroying our tourist industry and costing 50,000 British jobs this year alone.

'We've had a period in which people could get away with not being of the highest quality,' said Christopher Rodrigues, the chairman of VisitBritain. 'But we're now in an environment where you have to do quality. Poor value for money and poor service cost jobs, and will cost more jobs in a recession.' He went on to say that 'threadbare towels', 'a previously owned bar of soap' and 'a grumpy person who says "we don't do breakfast before 8 a.m. and we don't do it after 8.12 a.m."' will no longer be tolerated (I know, I know, 12 whole minutes for breakfast, he must have been thinking of the Ritz) and, effectively, that we are going to have to smile and serve and grovel our way out of the financial crisis.

All this by way of preparation for the prime minister's launch of a £6 million campaign to publicise how the collapse of sterling has made Britain more affordable for foreign tourists.

Doesn't it make you proud? Britain may be cold, miserable, rude and dirty, Gordon Brown seemed to be telling the world's holidaymakers, but at least it's cheap! Soon, presumably, impoverished Thai students will be backpacking round England with guidebooks telling them how to survive on two dollars a week. Rowdy Lithuanian bachelors will book stag parties in Park Lane because the booze and hookers are so ridiculously cheap, and Congolese tabloids will offer their readers £1 booze cruises to Folkestone. And they'll all go home staggered by the misery, rudeness and filth. With this in mind, I thought it would be a good time to issue some simple survival tips to foreign travellers coming to Britain this year:

1. Do not pay full price. When shopping in Britain, bear in mind that the price marked is only a guide; it is always best to haggle. Prices in Harrods, for example, may look ridiculously cheap to you, but locals cannot afford to pay even this much and if you pay more you will make life harder for them in the end. Do not damage their frail local economy with your powerful rupees.

2. When speaking to staff in shops, hotels and restaurants, do not expect them to be solicitous, kind or helpful. What do you think they are, your bleeding butler? Effing nerve. What did your last servant die of?

3. If you do decide to make some purchases, do not forget that Savile Row suits and shirts from Jermyn Street may seem incredibly good value and look great with a tan when you're in that holiday frame of mind, but all that ethnic tat can look pretty ridiculous when you get it home.

4. Never ask a salesperson for help finding an item in your size or preferred colour – they will merely stare at you blankly as if you are an escaped lunatic and then tell you that everyfink is out on the floor. If you absolutely insist that they go and check the stockroom they will walk round a random corner, count to 30 and then go on a tea break.

5. Do not expect to find a full range of products in shops. Most shops in Britain are in receivership and merely flogging off old stock before being boarded up.

6. If taken by locals to a restaurant such as Garfunkel's, Nando's, or any number of chain pubs offering

'Traditional Roast Dinner!!!' on a big red banner strung across the roof, do your best not to pull faces or vomit – for the natives, eating in these places is considered a treat.

7. Take a good supply of colourful pens with you to give to the children who will flock around you asking for presents. And if you want to be really popular then give them knives: British children treasure these more than anything.

8. Light bulbs, on the other hand, make great gifts for grown-ups, as the traditional British light bulb is being phased out by bleeding-heart environmental scaremongers who want to plunge Britain into darkness.

9. It is always important to carry a supply of clean needles when travelling, but if you are likely to find yourself in hospital while staying in Britain it is also advisable to pack a full body antiviral protection suit, anti-bacterial scrub-down unit, and, if you are going to be in overnight, a bed.

10. Do not be put off if the people appear cold or standoffish towards you. They are not even nice to each other unless they are being bombed.

11. Don't forget to take part in the national pastime of binge drinking. With the recession in danger of putting a stop to this great British tradition, the Wetherspoon pub chain has started offering pints of beer at 99p a go. 'Bottoms up!' – as they say when, after ten or eleven of these drinks, they drop their trousers and stand on their heads on the road outside.

The Retreat from 'Here'

It so happened one day that I was leafing through my morning newspaper and came upon two stories, only a few pages apart, which, although not presented as such, told a very similar tale about modern life, one with obvious comic implications, the other with tragic ones. Both were about dealing with modern teenagers, and both were about cars.

The first story began as follows: 'Haynes manuals, the bible of home car mechanics, are branching out to take on a particularly tricky and temperamental model – the teenager.' It went on to describe the technological advances that have made home car-maintenance a thing of the past and led the famous DIY car people to move into domestic and familial how-to publishing.

It's obvious, really, that the people whose advice about cars we no longer need should be the ones we turn to for help bringing up our children.

For example, if you have noticed your son is wearing his trousers round his knees and walking about with his left hand inside his underpants (as so many teenage boys do now), you can simply turn to the page where it says: 'Stupid Teenage Walks – a longstanding fault with the model. Simply tighten the fanbelt, sorry, waistband. Failing that, apply WD40 to all moving parts.'

If the kid listens to his iPod at dinner, drumming the table with his fingers and making infuriating nodding motions instead of eating: 'Try a jump-start. But remember to connect both positive and negative cable heads to your live 12v battery before applying to each ear of the teenager.' If the kid keeps saying 'like'

and 'innit' and 'blood' and repeatedly calls you 'motherf*****':
'Tap head sharply with the back of a screwdriver.'

If the kid starts doing crack and then gets pregnant: 'You've
been sold a duffer, check warranty and apply to manufacturer for
refund or replacement.'

Ha ha. Funny.

The other story began like this: 'A teenage motorist was
facing prison yesterday after admitting killing a pensioner while
sending a text on her mobile phone.' That's the tragic reprise. In
both stories, digital technology has brought about the death of
something: in the first, car manuals; in the second, a person.

Had digital technology not enabled the invention of the
mobile phone, the driver, Rachel Begg, might have been looking
where she was going. And the pensioner, Maureen Waites, 64,
might not have been killed.

Had digital technology not led to the computerisation of
the automobile engine and the superannuating of the relatively
simple traditional motor, people might still be mending their
cars at home, using manuals.

Taken together, both stories have great nostalgic potential.
One can't help imagining that in her youth Maureen Waites was
driven around 1950s and 60s Britain in cars made of steel and
smelling of leather, maintained by their owners with the help of
a broken-spined Haynes manual flopped open at the page with
the gearbox diagram.

Owners who, when they had done the best they could to get
the oil off their hands, called her up on a heavy bakelite phone,
turning the dial ponderously and waiting for it to return between
digits, to ask if she wanted to go out for a drive. Or even wrote a
note, in ink or pencil, to put through her door.

The car that hit hers will have weighed less than half what
those cars of her youth weighed. Its driver will never have looked
under its bonnet. Rachel Begg will have had as little idea how her

car works as her phone. But don't blame her for the killing. She wasn't even there.

The iPod that cuts off the kid from the aural community, the gobbing in the street, the mobile phone used to connect to elsewhere because 'here' is briefly tedious are all part of the same blurring of boundaries between private and public space. The abnegation of society. The retreat from 'here'.

Drivers who got to know their car through their Haynes manual were right there in the moment when they drove that car. Rachel Begg was completely elsewhere. In a world at the other end of a text message that contained neither her car, nor the road, nor Mrs Waites.

Both stories are about an atomised society. Fragmented ties. We are only as interested in our children as our parents were in their cars. Teenagers have gone a bit wrong, we know that. So we buy a manual (Haynes's *The Teenager Manual* by Dr Pat Spungin costs £14.99 and is available from, I imagine, bookshops) and promise to give them a tweak at the weekend. See if we can't get to the bottom of the strange whining noise. The funny smell.

But you can't fix teenagers with a textbook. It's too late for that. The modern teenager is as hardwired for incomprehensibility, solipsism and brutish collision with its environment as your new 4x4.

For all the benefits you no doubt believe it has also brought, the technology that killed the Haynes car manual also created our teenagers. And killed Mrs Waites.

Monocle

I can't tell you how furious I was when I first heard that Tyler Brûlé, the man behind *Wallpaper*, was to launch a new magazine called *Monocle*, not for the gay urban soft-furnishings nut this time, but for the rich. Just, the rich.

Monocle was to have offices in London, Tokyo, New York and Zurich (a rare example of the simple bracketing together of four cities being enough to make one want to vomit), and would 'aim to appeal to successful professionals who divide their time between several cities'. People with no soul, in other words. Men with monogrammed wheelie luggage who hunt money like Stone Age men hunted food – without moral question and brutishly, because they are intellectually underdeveloped and it is all they know.

But what baffled me most was the supposition that the rich constitute a single interest group and all want to read the same stuff, rather than being a lot of different individuals who just happen to have a lot of loot. Do they all like the same poems and novels as each other as well? And are they different novels and poems from the ones the rest of us like? Do truly loaded people slam the new Zadie Smith shut after thirty pages and mutter: 'I'm simply too wealthy for this rubbish'?

As it happens, I don't really think of the super-rich as being big readers of anything much at all. They are either too busy earning money to waste their time with words (which are just a consolation prize for those of us too poor to buy happiness) or, if they inherited their money, too feckless, or, if they got it from playing football or singing pop songs, too dim. So what would this magazine have in it?

People buy angling magazines or food magazines or porn magazines because they are interested in, and want to know more about, angling or food or impressively proportioned naughty bits and cutting-edge depilation. But richness, per se, isn't anything at all. It's like the idea of a magazine for nice people, or people who yawn not because they're tired but because they're nervous.

What is it that the Queen, Simon Cowell and Lakshmi Mittal have in common that would make them all want to read the same magazine? And why would Stephen Hawking, Bernie Ecclestone and Maeve Binchy like it too?

The only really super-rich person I know quite well is James Dyson, whose autobiography I co-wrote. He is worth, I am aware, many billions, but he's a slim chap who likes angora sweaters and salad, going for a run, watching a bit of rugby and holidaying in France. Admittedly, his car isn't rusty and he likes big houses, but it's hard to imagine him rushing out to the newsagent to buy a new periodical because he's heard it is very much enjoyed by Wayne Rooney, Cher and the fat younger brother of the Sultan of Brunei.

Monocle claims to focus on 'business coverage, reportage, cultural criticism and luxury goods'. Of these, it is the 'cultural criticism' to which I most look forward. The rich are so good at criticising cultures.

'Sub-Saharan Africa you can forget,' I imagine *Monocle* observing. 'The wine is terrible and they make crap yachts. The only thing worth buying here is orphans, which are available at very competitive rates. Babies are already getting pricier in the major cities, but if you're prepared to stray off the beaten track there are still some bargains to be had. Do remember, though, that while black children look very cute when young, they may, when older, be a bit of an embarrassment at the golf club. It is also a good idea to buy at least one more than you really need, as when you get them home everyone is going to be wanting one, and it's so nice, when a friend admires your child, to be able to give it to her.'

Interestingly, *Monocle* is published ten times a year. This may look odd to povvoes like you, who are used to magazine issue dates being more of a reflection of the way the calendar divides. But what you don't know is that your so-called 'months' are not good enough for the likes of Katie Price, Sting and the ginger kid out of *Harry Potter*. They use their own private months, such as Cashuary, Wongust and Moolarch, and these are so expensive that the year can only afford to have ten of them.

Best of all, *Monocle* announced at its launch that 'the title will sell for £5 and be printed on expensive paper', which may well be the naffest sentence I've ever read. What does 'expensive paper' do that 'sensibly priced paper' doesn't? Does it read itself? Does it twist itself, when you've finished with it, into handy little firelighters for the hearth in the east wing dining room? Does it wipe itself clean of the drool that falls from your hanging gob when you're gawping at adverts for matching luggage?

And isn't five quid rather a lot? I look forward, as copycat magazines attempt to muscle in on this lucrative market (with names like *Cufflink*, *Moneyclip* and *Tiepin*), to a savage price-cutting war. I'm sure I could bring such a mag in at, say, £4.52. And don't tell me that the likes of Rupert Murdoch, Ronan Keating and the thirteen wives of the King of Swaziland don't know the difference between paying a fiver for a lot of preliterate advertorial and photos of yachts, and paying a fiver for a lot of preliterate advertorial and photos of yachts, a packet of pickled-onion Monster Munch and three Cola Chews.

Debrett's Etiquette for Girls

You may or may not have heard already about the most recent addition to the Debrett's library of social reference guides, *Etiquette for Girls*. If you have, then that is probably because you are a long-time consumer of Debrett's books, take a great interest in polite behaviour and will be too polite to say so. And if you haven't, then brace yourselves.

For the new guide is not a set of lessons in how to climb into a hackney carriage without offering so much as a glimpse of one's – whoops! Is that the time? Must be getting along. Nor is it about how to pin a Big Mac to your head at Ascot and persuade people it's a hat. Oh no. It seems that the time when girls worried their pretty little heads about such delicate things is past.

Nor has this new departure anything much to do with the (yawn) changing role of women in today's equal opportunities workplace. The etiquette advice is still all about the business of mating, much as it ever was; it is just that rather than focusing on the merry premarital dance once played out by fully clad young women, wide-eyed and waiting for the wedding before finally (and this was always the ultimate objective) dropping their knickers, the new Debrett's rather portrays the modern (upper-middle class, let's face it) young woman as frantically scuttling around town with her knickers round her ankles from pretty much the end of her GCSEs until miserable, shagged-out middle age.

'If you're the "other woman",' drawls the book, wearily,

defeatedly, simply accepting immorality, depravity and sexual incontinence as a given, 'remember not to get too involved: a married man rarely leaves his wife.'

Should you be in it just for the shagging, though, which Debrett's clearly thinks is the more sensible attitude, then you are advised to 'avoid dark-alley gropery and unladylike fumbling in the back of a cab'.

'Avoid dark-alley gropery?' Is that etiquette? Blimey. All that means is, 'Don't drop your pants till you get in his front door.'

It seems a sad admission that decency is over and ladies have gone to crap. For example, after first reducing the phrase 'one-night stand' to the chortlesome faux-toff acronym 'ONS' (because, obviously, this book is going to be talking so frequently about the tricky business of screwing a man you've never met before that it needs some shorthand), *Etiquette for Girls* explains that: 'The ONS isn't over until the following morning's "walk of shame" home in last night's outfit. Steel yourself and hold your head up high. At yours, offer him breakfast and (assuming you want no more of him) say that your mother is on her way round.'

Hell and goddam. Can this advice on how to rid yourself of last night's portion of no-longer-needed cock by casual invocation of your dear mother's name really be coming from the people who, until relatively recently, existed only to tell us where at the table to seat a duchess if the archbishop is deaf in one ear and has to sit on the baronet's left?

Leaving decency aside (and they clearly have), what I don't understand is why Debrett's is under the impression that girls, specifically, need their own set of rules. Girls, of all people. From my experience, women's heads are so full of bizarre rules gleaned from magazines and self-help books, about everything from which wine to take to a dinner party given by a chef to how to give a blow job on a bus, that they hardly dare sneeze without first looking up how to do it in *Cosmo*.

Isn't etiquette supposed to be universal? Isn't the point of good behaviour that if we all do it, and abide by the same rules, then everything will go smoothly? As soon as you start offering a different set of rules to each individual social group, then you lose the civilising effect of everybody pulling in the same direction for the common interest.

What are Debrett's going to offer us next? Debrett's *Etiquette for Hoodies*? I can well imagine it: 'When dressing for the shopping centre after midnight remember: one simply doesn't wear a brown hood in town.

'In the matter of footwear, don't forget the old adage "white is right".

'When gobbing on a pavement it is considered meet to create a great rasping sound as you hawk up the phlegm, in order that as many people as possible may observe the act.

'Knife wearing: when packing a blade, it is generally the form these days to conceal it from view. But the rule here is "only draw it if you plan to use it". Pulling it out and merely waving it around will make you a laughing stock. At Debrett's we have a little mnemonic: "Draw, and stab". It's that easy: "Draw, and stab", "Draw and stab".'

And how about Debrett's *Etiquette for Professional Drivers*?: 'On first noticing a bird with a fat pair of jubblies and nipples you could hang your hat on, it is not the form to wind down one's window and shout "tits out for the lads" then honk like a sea lion.

'In the first instance, a double tap on the horn is polite. Should she turn and acknowledge the interruption, you may then press on with the dialogue, perhaps using some witticism to break the ice such as betting her that she does not get many of them to the pound.

'Should she fail to acknowledge you, however, it is generally considered fitting to call her a miserable cow, and advise her to cheer up, on the grounds that whatever it is she is worrying about may never happen.'

Footballers

A charity called RoadPeace has criticised the Transport Department for collaborating with the Football League in a road safety campaign, because footballers are such demonstrably bad and dangerous drivers. If footballers are committed to road safety, says the group, 'they should lead by example and drive small, safe cars and make a commitment not to speed and to drive safely'.

Hmmm. I'm just trying to picture it. I'm trying to see a 19-year-old wunderscally celebrating his £40 million move to Manchester United (in a deal that gives him £200,000 a week, plus three helicopters and as many go-go-dancing Danish virgins as he can eat) by going out and buying a brand-new Ford Ka. Or Honda Civic. Or Seat Ibiza (with cigarette lighter and passenger-side vanity mirror).

I'm trying to see the front page of *Hello!* screaming its exclusive photos of 'David Beckham at home with his stunning collection of economical yet surprisingly capacious one-litre hatchbacks'.

I'm trying to see headlines like: 'Premiership star arrested for driving too slowly on dual carriageway in hydrogen-powered eco-buggy' and 'Ronaldo prangs bicycle again – basket irreparable.' And I'm having a bit of trouble.

A typical example of the way footballers think about cars was the response of Les Ferdinand, Ferrari collector and former occasional scorer of fluky goals with his knee, to an interviewer who asked him if he was a safe driver. 'I drive fast, but safely,'

Ferdinand said, missing the point of safe driving as howlingly as ever he missed a sitter in the six-yard box with the scores level in extra time and the keeper lying unconscious on the touchline.

But Ferdinand just wasn't going to say: 'Yes, I drive well within the limits of human reaction time, taking my lead from prevailing road conditions. I know my stopping distances by heart, always wear a seatbelt, and am so averse to high speeds that I could get a nosebleed taking a sharp corner in a milk float.' Because, if he did, he would get no respect from his pig-ignorant, villainous, oafish peers.

Footballers are witless, illiterate, spoilt morons who are no good at driving because they are no good at anything at all, except, very occasionally, playing football, and then only if they are French.

They can't speak, they can't read, they need *Sun* journalists (God help them) to write their autobiographies for them; they can't hold their alcohol, they can't have a relationship with a woman without beating her, they can't remember to show up at a drugs test unless their mummy takes them, they can't organise a strike properly or avoid injury before big internationals, and they can't tell a well-cut suit from an empty pantomime horse.

Footballers are the apogee of the modern British male as fêted by men's magazines, late-night television programming and advertisers of almost every stripe – for they understand only money, lewdness and brutality. They converse in the vulgar patois of cars, tits and speed. For Christ's sake, these people think that Graeme Le Saux is gay because he reads *The Guardian*. What would they do if he bought a VW Beetle?

The sportswriter Brian Glanville has been knocked about for explaining the problems encountered by some footballers in a radio interview in the following terms: 'They have very little education and then suddenly these uneducated boys are projected into a world in which they are earning £40,000 or £50,000 a week; there are no controls.'

The uproar was because Brian was talking about black players, but the degeneracy of footballers has nothing to do with race or environment. All footballers are scumbags. Black, white, or yell— no, wait, those Japanese and Korean chaps at the World Cup were rather marvellous. They probably had degrees.

But RoadPeace is right. Footballers should be stopped from driving their stupid sports cars. Not because of the bad example they set in the field of road safety but because of the bad example they set in everything.

In the days when footballers only very occasionally became famous, it did not matter that they were, without exception vain, crass and moronic. The odd George Best or Charlie Nicholas came to the fore, but the rest we saw only occasionally, clumping around in the mud on a Saturday afternoon. Now that all footballers are famous, something has to be done.

So, yes, ban them from owning fast cars. But ban them also from living in gated mock-Tudor estates, ban them from going to nightclubs, ban them from spitting, ban them from beating up Asian students, ban them from saying 'as I say' all the time, ban them from buying Versace frock coats and ties the same colour as their shirts, ban them from owning vast plasma-screen televisions and Bang & Olufsen stereos but no books, ban them from keeping pedigree dogs called 'Prince' and 'Lady', ban them from calling their children 'Dene' and 'Chenille', ban them from going out with ropey peroxided media tarts, and ban them from punching them, ban them from listening to soul music, ban them from writing naff messages on their vests and then tearing off their shirts in public, ban them from doing their special 'celebrations' and then explaining them to the press afterwards, ban them from using the historic present tense, wearing jewellery and raping young women, from taking bungs and dyeing their hair and calling people 'gaffer'.

Lock them up and let them out only on Saturdays, when it is time for them to perform, like the depraved, venal, punch-drunk circus animals they are.

Anorexia Hysteria

Asked during an interview with a fashion website if she had any mottos, Kate Moss replied, 'Nothing tastes as good as skinny feels'. And the clouds parted, and the sky opened, and Hell rained down upon her.

'Outrage over Kate's size zero motto', screamed one newspaper. 'Storm at "anorexia" comments', cried another, putting 'anorexia' in inverted commas, of course, because Kate didn't say anything about anorexia at all.

Most of the time the tabloids lambast Kate for the twin evils of endorsing drug abuse and taking pleasure from sexual intercourse, but this time they were furious because, by apparently celebrating a lifestyle choice which involves exercising willpower in the face of temptation in order to feel good about herself, Kate is, of course, encouraging teenage girls to develop a mental illness and die.

It's so stupid and hysterical and infuriating I don't know where to start.

It is quite tempting to start with the disastrous collapse of journalistic standards – largely thanks to bloggorrhoea, the web generally, and the Cowellisation of our culture – that leads a journalist (working for an apparently very widely read and respected website called *Women's Wear Daily*) to ask one of the world's most famous (and undeniably powerful) women a question as facile and dim-witted as 'What's your motto?'

In Kate's shoes (yummy), I'd have said, 'My motto is "don't waste time talking to website imbeciles whose attention span runs no further than the length of a word-belch on Twitter"' and hung up.

But Kate is not like that. Kate thought for a minute and then decided to say something that dovetails with her profile, is quite funny, and is completely, utterly true.

Of course being thin is better than being fat. (The very paper that was 'outraged' by Kate's comments on page 21 ran an interview on page 53 celebrating the weight-loss achievements of a *Casualty* actress under the headline: 'Anyone who says they're fat and happy is lying. And I should know. I went from this . . . to this . . .' alongside a grotesque 'before' picture of a woman you could render down to grease a fleet of battleships, and an 'after' pic of a woman not much bigger than Kate Moss.)

And they were right the second time. 'Fat and happy' is a myth, a monstrous lie, and I thoroughly endorse Kate's statement. I don't eat anything like as much as I'd like to – despite eating for a living – because I don't want to be fat. And if my saying that leads half a dozen boys to stop eating until they die because they want to be like me, well then, frankly, those are boys we're probably better off without.

I long to be skinny. I'd die to be skinny. As it is, I content myself with a borderline OK BMI because I can't manage any better. I simply don't have Kate's staggering willpower. But I try. I weigh myself half a dozen times every morning (before I pee, then afterwards, then left foot first, then right foot first – which, bizarrely, seems to give a different reading – then pre-poo, then post-poo, then again if I so much as blow my nose or trim my beard) and then determine how much I'm allowed to eat today accordingly: if I'm under 12 stone 7 pounds then I can eat pretty much anything. If I'm over that then I deduct a thousand calories for each pound I'm over, and if I've crept to 12 stone 10 pounds then I eat nothing at all and go for an hour-long run on the Heath, taking the hills as fast as I can – which will make me feel sick, with a bit of luck, and not want to eat.

I was chubbyish once, and miserable as hell – this would be ten years ago – then I lost a bit of weight, a stone maybe, and,

Pow! Happiness. Pay rise, lots of cute girls, TV career. It's not rocket science. And the only way to lose weight and keep it off effectively is to develop a sense of the long-term as opposed to short-term effects of everything you eat. The ability to act with future as opposed to immediate wellbeing in mind is one of the defining mental strengths of the human.

As such, Kate's apparently simple philosophy is wonderfully advanced and extremely timely. To every action there is a consequence, that is all she is saying. But it is something that is being increasingly forgotten in our instant-gratification, bling-bling, *X Factor*, fizzy pop, white bread world. Kate owes all she has to her shape, and she accepts the acts of denial on which that shape depends. Cigarettes, hard drugs and (it is said) orgies, are all things that do not appear to do her any harm, so she feels no need to eschew them. Lucky girl. I wish I was made of the same stuff. She is an absolute icon of willpower, self-knowledge and strength – she is cut from the same cloth as the brave Tommies who won us two world wars.

The wider application of Kate's consequence-aware behavioural code might see impressionable young people being told, 'No drunken night out with the girls is as fun as not being raped by an unlicensed minicab driver and left for dead in a grimy back street', or, 'no summer of bunking off and smoking joints in the park when you should be revising for your GCSEs is as much fun as a life spent not being a dustman.'

The message that every action in life has a consequence is a glorious and honourable one to propound.

Apart from anything else, what we have in the developed world is an obesity crisis, not an anorexia crisis. Sure, it is sad that a handful of young women harm themselves every year in the pursuit of the size zero mirage, but it is nothing compared to the 100,000 Britons who die every year from diseases related to obesity. If Kate's bon mots are really so influential that they will stop people eating, reverse the obesity tide (especially in children), save the £4 billion a year lost to the national purse as a consequence of mass fatness, and bring our life expectancy averages back on track then, frankly, a few unhappy teenagers is a small price to pay.

And anyway, Kate is only being honest. She is admitting that to look the way she does she has to not eat. That is a much less dangerous message to young girls than all those models who claim to eat normally. 'I love fast food, especially burgers', most models say in interviews, trying to seem normal, 'and I'm forever bingeing on chocolate'. But the truth is they have livid skin, foul breath and hairy backs because not a morsel passes their lips from one week to the next. These sour-faced, lying vixens are the ones who are making young girls on healthy diets think there must be something wrong with them. Not honest Kate.

I did a lame-arse television food quiz in the summer with, among others, the theoretically more womanly-sized supermodel Sophie Dahl. At one point Hugh Fearnley-Whittingstall handed round a bag of cherries. We all tucked in. Afterwards, the more-than-womanly-sized Clarissa Dickson Wright gestured towards the lovely Sophie, who now has her own cookery show, and said, 'That's the first time I have ever seen someone taking bites out of a cherry.'

'Hope All Is Well with You'

Hi. Hope all is well with you. I've just read the thrilling news that Abi Titmuss is to play Lady Macbeth at the Seagull Theatre, Lowestoft, and it got me to thinking about just what in the world is . . . hang on, what happened there? Don't tell me I began by saying that I hope all is well with you. Oh no, I did.

I can hardly be blamed. It's the first sentence of every email I ever read, and I suppose it must be contagious. But where on earth did it come from? Every email I get, whether it's a commission from a newspaper or magazine, a letter from my bank, a reminder from the gas company or a cunning financial plan from West Africa, begins, 'Hi,' or 'Dear Giles' or (very, very rarely) 'Dear Mr Coren', and then, 'Hope all is well with you.'

I have just this minute, for example, deleted an email from the master of a Cambridge college asking me to come and talk about sustainable food systems, gratis and without fee, to a roomful of goggling nano-boffins, which began 'Dear Giles, hope all is well with you.'

In the first place, how come 'Giles'? I've never met the four-eyed conehead. Can they not bring themselves, even in tank-top-wearing, cycle-crazy, straight As, gowns-for-dinner, saving-myself-till-I'm-married Cambridge, to call a man they've never met 'Mr'? It's a wonder Professor Bumstorm (as I'll call him to save his blushes) didn't go the whole hog and address me as 'Giley'.

But that's not my grumble. My grumble is this awful, throwaway, 'Hope all is well with you' thing they insist on opening with. Why do they hope that all is well with me? Not for my sake, I'll wager, but for theirs. My dozens of daily unmet well-wishers are hoping that I am not lying slumped and cold on the floor of my downstairs loo because then I won't be able to write a feature for their stupid magazine about the death of the dinner party, or give them a spell of work experience, or send them a cheque for fifty grand so as to free up millions further down the line, or come and eat a terrible dinner in their draughty craphole of a college.

I suppose they feel that they have to say something vaguely me-related and polite, because it might sound in some way rude to just start in with what they're trying to wheedle out of me. It's like the endless internal emails that come to 'all *Times* users', which used to be very rare and always began 'I'm really sorry to bother you with one of these infuriating "global emails", but I've tried all my contacts and just can't seem to get a lead – has anyone got a contact number for Fidel Castro's proctologist?' which now come at least six times an hour and just say 'Usual apologies, anyone got a Pritt stick?' But that's not an apology! And you need to apologise to me, because it drives me up the wall here in Kentish Town, permanently logged on to *The Times* email system as I am, always rummaging in my drawers for the required item and then worrying how on earth I'm going to get it across town to Wapping in time to avert what is clearly a major crisis.

But 'Hope all is well with you' is even worse. For what it seeks to do is to establish a theoretical mood plane on which you are currently buzzing along like a happy bee, untroubled by the woes of the world, almost certainly having a better time than your correspondent, in a state from which it would be impossible to say no to whatever he or she wants.

If, they reason, you happen to be recovering from major heart surgery at the present time, then you can be forgiven for being unenthusiastic about running a half-marathon in Battersea Park on Sunday to raise money for the local school's 'Buy every pupil a cormorant' campaign. But if all is well with you, well then, put on your trainers, man, and stop snivelling!

But it all rather depends on how you define 'well'. Are you worried about something big that you might not have heard about on account of your not being quite in the thick of my private wellness loop?

Are you worried that I may recently have been diagnosed with cancer, lost my job or mislaid a favourite pet? Or perhaps that my girlfriend passed away in the night and that I awoke this morning to find her stiff corpse gathering flies beside me in the bed, and therefore, having logged on regardless, to check my emails and do a bit of Twittering, may think it rude if you do not account for the possibility in your opening line? And that my fury at your failure to acknowledge that all might not be well with me might make me less likely to visit your restaurant with a view to writing a review/give your daughter a job/recommend a keenly priced Mongolian grill with a good buzz, sensible wine-list and good music not too far from Snaresbrook Tube?

Who knows? Luckily, Esther made it through the night, and so all is well on that front. I also woke up this morning myself, so that was a bonus. I had breakfast without choking on a nut and followed up with a satisfactory bowel movement. You could call that a hell of a morning, if you liked. But when you say 'all' . . . I mean, how deeply do you want me to reflect?

For example, I am forty years old and creak more grievously every morning. I played fives last night and by the end of a match in which I was comfortably the worst (because the oldest) player on court I could barely walk. I have a lot of work to do, not all of it very appealing. I have just wasted 20 minutes of my morning trying to get through to Abbey National (whose automated voice line was interested only in repeatedly telling me that they would soon be changing their name to Santander, as if anyone in the world, as long as he is getting a half-decent mortgage rate, is going to care what name his building society uses to introduce itself at parties), so that I could transfer some more of my life savings into a current account to pay the builders I hired in April and was hoping would be out by June but who are currently downstairs relaying the cloakroom lino for the fourteenth time because they still haven't managed to cut the right shape to get it flush with the bog-bowl stand.

I have people coming to dinner tonight, one of whom has just revealed that his girlfriend is a vegan, and another of whom wants to bring his mother. The industry in which I have worked these last 17 years is practically on its knees and even the most optimistic projections say that I will be working in a call centre by the time I am 45, which is also the age at which, having dithered and dithered these last 20 years, I may finally get around to having children, who will never know me as anything but a decrepit old man who died of old age before they left school, so, no, ALL IS NOT WELL WITH ME.

And what are you going to do about it? Are you going to send flowers? Are you going to remember me in your prayers? Or are you just going to press on with whatever the hell barefaced piece of baldarse beggary you had in mind?

Anyway, so. Abi Titmuss is to play Lady Macbeth. Whatever.

The Fattest Man in the World

Hussein Bolt, the world's fastest man, may be Jamaican. Warren Buffett and Bill Gates, the world's richest men, may both be American. Australia will always have the most impressive sheep-to-man ratio on earth and nobody will beat the Germans for beer drinking. But at least Britain has Paul Mason, who was unearthed this week as very possibly the fattest person in the world.

In these post-Imperial days, when ideas of Britain's greatness have receded into distant memory, world exploration has become a joke (mostly about Ranulph Fiennes's toes), the human genome has been mapped, the source of the Nile discovered and Cheryl Cole's hair has achieved a glossiness from her shampoo once unimaginable without a visit to a salon, people were beginning to ask what peaks were left for man to scale, what lands to conquer.

And then, from nowhere, an Englishman weighed in at 70 stone (displacing the previous record holder, who shed half his bodyweight in preparation for his marriage to some lucky, lucky girl) and restored a little national pride.

To be the world's heaviest man is one of the great records. The long-time holder of the title, the 52-stone pre-Victorian porker Daniel Lambert, was always, for me, right up there with the fastest and the richest and the tallest of humans. Tall is good, too, but Robert Pershing Wadlow, the 8-foot 11-inch giant from Illinois, secured his place in the record books thanks to hypertrophy of the pituitary gland. Dumb luck, in other words.

Lambert, on the other hand, did it all himself. And his

achievement was of a different order. To be the world's tallest man was a thing I knew (just from looking around at family functions) that I could never achieve. But to be the world's fattest, why, that was an ambition available to any red-blooded kid with a healthy appetite and the capacity to dream.

Lambert was such a splendid fellow in his frock coat, high weskit, stock and white gaiters – a Regency dandy to the power of ten. And of course the late 18th century was a time when being fat was, if not quite fashionable, certainly not the indicator of material and spiritual poverty it is today. The Prince Regent was fat. Louis XVI was positively humungous. On reaching 50 stone, Lambert commissioned a special cart and headed down from Leicester to London where he charged people a shilling a go to look at him. Marvellous.

Paul Mason needs special transport, too. It's how he first came to media attention this week, with the headline 'World's Heaviest Man requires Chinook airlift for life-saving operation'. It sounded funny for some reason. Maybe it's the word 'Chinook', or maybe it's the image of this giant fatty swinging from a military helicopter over the English countryside. But it's certainly something to get a laugh from a sentence with 'life-saving operation' in it.

But poor old Paul Mason really isn't funny or marvellous at all. I met him in 2006 when I was making a documentary about obesity. Back then, at a mere 47 stone, he was not yet the fattest man in Britain, let alone the world. He may not even have been the fattest man in Ipswich. But, unlike the others, he was prepared to see us. For a fee, of course – £200, I think it was. Lambert would have approved.

But Paul Mason by no means cut the dash that I always imagined Lambert did. Walking into the airless, moist, very close and dimly lit room in which he lived – in temporary accommodation while a specially appointed bungalow was being built for him at taxpayer's expense – I did not allow the horror that welled up in me to express itself as visitors to Lambert would have done, with their insensitive 18th-century ways.

And so I did not yell, 'Somebody call Greenpeace! We'll have to roll him back out to sea on the next tide!' when I came upon Mason, beached in the giant bed from which he had not stirred in nine years, laptop, television controls and tubs of fizzy pop in easy reach, toy daleks conveniently placed on a nearby shelf, his small, grey, sad little head bobbing on the sea of fat that was his body.

I just said, 'Hello, I'm Giles,' and shook his great mitten of a hand, like squeezing a cold hot-water bottle.

I was there to confront him with my (not altogether serious) plan to tackle the obesity crisis by taxing fat people directly so as to recoup some of the £4 billion that obesity costs the nation each year, and to offer fat people a financial incentive to change. Not including his special accommodation, Paul costs Suffolk Health Authority £100,000 a year to keep alive. And they had recently invested another £100,000 in a special ambulance to enable him to get to hospital (previously, two fire crews had been needed).

But it was very hard to do. All my fight and bluster, all my anger at the hopelessness of fat people went out of me. The room was so depressing, the reality so bleak, the man so pitiful. So I went all third person and said: 'There are probably people who would want to know why they should have to foot the bill for people like you.'

'It's one of the things that eats away inside of you,' he said, in his quiet Ipswich accent, his little mouth moving in the middle of his huge face, like something superimposed by clever animation. 'Why should they spend money on you, right? When you see other cases around which are more deserving. Something has to be done. But we can't do it. Can't physically do it. But why should the money be spent? The way I look at it is because I'm a human being. I have human being rights. I never made myself like this. I didn't want to be like this.'

It was awful. Even as he moaned that he was a human being I was thinking how much less like a human being he looked than any human being I had ever seen. He wasn't protesting that he was a 'man' or even a 'human'. He was asking only that I recognise his membership of the species. His being a 'being'. Existing at all. That was the summit of his pride.

Paul's super-obesity was probably linked to depression, which was probably linked to unemployment, which was definitely linked to his having gone to prison for stealing money from letters while working as a postman. But he had abrogated all responsibility for his condition now, and was most comfortable casting himself as a victim (or even, with his toys and his pyjamas and his sugary snacks, as a helpless child).

Paul Mason may well find his way into the next *Guinness Book of Records* alongside Daniel Lambert, and schoolboys will no doubt goggle at the details of his size. But he would fit just as easily onto the page for 'most hopeless man in the world', if one were required – his giant size as lucid a reflection of his utterly defeated nature as any fat person's has ever been.

When I was finished with my questions and a researcher had handed him his envelope of cash ('don't spend it all on sweeties . . .'), Paul put the diagrams of his special bungalow (such a depressing phrase: 'special bungalow') back into their plastic folder and laid it on the table at his elbow.

On the back of it was a notice he had written in blue biro which read: 'If you are a new carer: please don't give me any biscuits. No matter how much I ask.'

The Super-Clever

In common with almost everyone you will meet, apart from lawyers, I have very little interest in the law. It exists, so far as I can fathom, only to provide a lifetime of homework for Oxbridge over-achievers whose sense of self-worth is so bound up in getting their prep done and passing their exams that, were these twin elements of student life to be denied them after their education was over, they would simply shrivel up and die.

Like the shark that must keep swimming or suffocate, lawyers are people who must stay in sub-fusc for ever, slinking from one crepuscular book-depository to the next, always reading, always note-taking, always worrying about what questions will come up, always worrying that the other guy will have done more work, have sharper pencils, will call for more paper first . . . and if the dawn should rise, and he is not safely tucked up in a library then – pfffst! – he turns into a bat. (Assuming, of course, that 'pfffst!' is the noise a lawyer makes upon turning into a bat. I have never actually been there to hear it happen, I confess, and thus have to assume it sounds a bit like someone opening a can of Lilt.)

But I did sit up and take notice when I read a piece from our legal editor headlined 'Brain "size of planet" is not big enough for top court, say judges'. Alongside was a photo of an affable-looking grey-hair leaning on his desk (as they always do) in front of a wall of old books (as they always are) with a file open in front of him (as one always is) and his reading glasses lying alongside (as a pair will always be).

'Ooh, old books bound in leather that nobody has ever

opened . . .' I thought. 'This chap must be HUMUNGOUSLY brainy!'

And I read on to learn that Jonathan Sumption, QC, IQ, ££, has applied for a place on the new Supreme Court but been strongly opposed by senior judges despite being described as having 'a brain the size of a planet'.

And I say, hurrah for those senior judges. Not because I think Mr Sumption, QC, IQ, ££, wouldn't do a good job, or that he is not very clever (he's a medieval historian *as well* as a top barrister – we're talking Rumpole meets R.J. Unstead here), but because what on earth use is a brain the size of a planet to anyone?

It won't fit in your head properly, for a start. And so there are bound to be headaches, sleeplessness, unpleasant leakages, all sorts. It's an interesting simile, though. As if sheer cell volume were a guarantee of intellect, rather than anything qualitative. Ted Danson, for example, the former *Cheers* barman and timeless star of *Three Men and a Baby*, has a massive head. Much bigger than Sumption's. So he probably has a bigger brain. Do you want him in your Supreme Court as well?

Usually, when thick people are trying to describe the cleverness of some egghead with dozens of consecutive degrees (although anyone can take several degree courses one after the other, it's just a matter of having the time), they go for quantity rather than volume.

I can't tell you the number of hacks who have passed through the doors of *The Times* with the informal middle name of 'Two Brains', 'Three Brains' or, most impressively, 'Four Brains' – due to their having tacked a couple of pointless years of 'research' onto the end of their common-or-garden Oxbridge degrees.

These multi-brains are evident in most walks of life (apart from football, where two A level passes famously earned Trevor Brooking the nickname 'The Professor'), and usually it is just people with big heads, or with the appearance of a big head due to a receding hairline. One thinks of David 'Five Brains'

Willetts or Alain 'Seven Brains' de 'Maybe Even Eight Brains' Botton.

Now, I have known Alain a long time. He is no thicko. But is he truly all that much smarter than, say, Stephen Fry? We'll never know, because Stephen has all his hair. But just imagine how clever we'd think Fry was if he went bald. Mind you, just imagine how depressed he would be.

Aaaaanyway, what was my point here? Er, hell, I've forgotten. Me and my blasted midget brain. Oh, I know, it was the pointlessness of being extremely clever.

For that is what these senior judges have, very bravely, expressed in the vetoing of Sumption: the fact that it's worth being clever, but only up to a point. Mycroft Holmes was cleverer than his brother, Sherlock. But who had the great flat in Baker Street, the awesome book deal, the film career . . . ? Who remembers what kind of hat Mycroft wore? Indeed, who even knows the name of the myopic, burbling boffin in *The Simpsons*?

I was quite clever as a kid. Perfectly clever enough to pass exams, get into good schools and universities, and get a job. But there it stopped. The very cleverest boys (single-sex education, sorry, can't extrapolate to the ladies), the ones who knew their 37x tables, read books that weren't on the syllabus, nailed the top scholarship positions and had all sorts of nervous rashes, eating disorders and orthopaedic spectacles, are the ones who have killed themselves, flunked out of top-level physics at 19 and live on the street, or ended up as commercial barristers.

It is what, according to Tuesday's comment pages, Roger Scruton wants for his children. 'TV will never poison my children's minds,' he wrote. 'They pursue old-fashioned habits such as talking, reading, riding and playing the piano. Brains subject to the wrong input in early years will be wrongly wired; vital capacities, both intellectual and emotional, will fail to be acquired, and the result will be a stunted human being.' Yoicks. That'll be a fun home to grow up in.

I should know, I had something similar going on as a kid. Not a total TV ban but a ration of five hours a week, to be selected in advance, at the beginning the week, by ringing the chosen items in the *Radio Times*, with no midweek changes allowed. Not that I'd have wanted to change. The selection was a no-brainer (luckily): Two-and-a-half hours of *Multi-Coloured Swap Shop*; *Match of the Day*; *The Six Million Dollar Man* and whichever out of *The Lone Ranger* and *Champion the Wonder Horse* was showing an episode I'd seen fewer than 30 times.

My parents imposed this because they wanted me to be clever. And it worked very well. I began reading, took an interest in maths, did my piano practice, started coming top in everything, and sailed through exams at the top of the year from 15 through to 21.

But when I left university I couldn't get a job. I was too clever. And too damn weird. So I turned the box on, got hip to *Neighbours* and *Home and Away* and *Fifteen to One*, stopped reading books altogether, started eating with my elbows on the table and moving my lips when reading road signs, and pretty soon I was a reasonably successful journalist, author and television presenter.

In the modern world, massive brains are a handicap. Look at the Nobel Peace Prize: time was they used to give it to people like Albert Schweitzer or Norman Borlaug, now it just goes to the good-looking guy whom everyone likes, even if he doesn't really know anything or do anything.

And that can only be good. These days, my brain is down to the size of a hazelnut, but it fits in my head a whole lot more comfortably than a planet.

Barcodes

I think we are all well aware that 7 October 2009 saw the 57th anniversary of the invention of the barcode. It's bizarre that we are, because it was hardly the most interesting thing about 7 October 2009, which was also, as you probably know, the 438th anniversary of the Battle of Lepanto, Heinrich Himmler's 109th birthday and the 97th anniversary (to the very day!) of the first transaction made on the Helsinki Stock Exchange. But it is the glorious 57th of the barcode that we know about.

And we know about it, of course, because Google decided to commemorate it in their 'doodle' du jour. And that is how we come to collectively know things about our days now. Once, it was the church calendar that told us: everyone knew intuitively that it was Whitsuntide, Ash Wednesday or Michaelmas. Then it was newspapers, and we all knew what the headlines were. And then it was television, and we all knew that tonight we'd find out who shot JR. But now it's whatever the hell some Korean kid in Silicon Valley feels like commemorating in a search engine logo doodle.

And so eight billion people, more or less, got up on Wednesday, logged on, saw a barcode where the multi-coloured 'Google' normally is, and thought, 'Eh? What's that? Oh, right, it must be the anniversary of the barcode. And that's probably "Google" written as a barcode.'

And how right we all were. And then I bet we all thought to ourselves, 'I wonder when it was invented? 1970-ish? Maybe mid-1960s at a push?', and were astounded when we clicked on the image for more information and found that it was invented, in fact, way back in 1952.

'1952?' we all probably screamed. 'That was coronation year! People in England barely had televisions, let alone barcode scanners! The very notion of the "shop" was still pretty much in its infancy. Most people in England were still driving their geese to market on Saturday mornings, hoping to exchange some of the feathers for a turnip and a quill. And in America they already had barcodes!'

No doubt you, like me, have thought since last Wednesday of practically nothing but barcodes (unless you are Vladimir Putin, who was also 57 on Wednesday and was probably too excited about all the cake and presents to notice). First of all I thought, 'What's so big about the 57th anniversary? Has Google, with all its binary programming and innovative teccy numerical stuff, simply done away with base 10 and its hidebound 'gold', 'silver' and 'diamond' anniversarial demarcations, and now the big one is really the 57th, or 'large lump of grit', anniversary?

And then, like me, I am certain you gave a moment's thought to the two chaps who (we learn) invented it, Norman Joseph Woodland and Bernard Silver. Such wonderfully evocative American names, so perfectly representative of opposite sides of the 'Dream'. It's so immediately obvious that good old Norman Woodland ('Norm!') was the one who came up with the idea for writing words as a sequence of lines, but that he had no head for business and only thought it might make a useful labelling system for Auntie May's apple pie stall at the barn-raising. And it was only when clever little Bernie Silver shuffled in on the act that they developed a plan to make money out of it.

It seems a rum thing to celebrate, though. Because what, after all, have we gained by the invention of the barcode (which, in the end, was first employed in a supermarket in Troy, Ohio, in 1974)?

As far as I can tell, the main thing the barcode has achieved is to have brought an end to the old-fashioned scenario in one's local shop, where the little man in the white overalls smiles as he takes down the flour tin from the shelf to weigh out your half pound, and says: 'Baking today, is it, Mrs Foskett? Not your famous fairy cakes? Hope there's one left over for me!'

Good work, barcode. You've certainly seen off that nosey old bastard.

Yup, the barcode killed the shop. Nice one. Like all modernising inventions, it came along with a brief to speed things up and, where possible, eradicate people. A bit like the industrialised Nazi death camps (happy birthday, Heinrich!). And while that may be great as a model for business or genocide, it rather runs counter to the instinctive will of humanity.

I tell a lie. The barcode did give us something useful. It gave us the phrase 'supermarket checkout girl' as a convenient shorthand for a girl of low status and minimal intellect – the sort of girl you don't want to end up settling for, or, if you are a girl, end up being. Whichever it is, she's waiting for you if you don't get on with your homework.

Swipe, swipe, blip. Swipe, swipe, blip. It's the sound of the end of the world. The final, total automation of the need to eat. The digitisation of the life instinct. Indeed, there are now supermarkets with no checkout staff at all, where you just swipe, swipe, blip the barcodes yourself, and go home without speaking a word. Such places are generally full of lonely singletons buying frozen lasagne and soft porn, rapists, and teenage muggers helping themselves to the booze. Good on you, Norman Jo! Hats off, Bernie!

And even if you are on the side of corporate rapine, and celebrate the bypassing of the human in all commercial transactions, wouldn't you have been more excited about 7 October if barcodes actually worked? If it wasn't always a case of some illiterate till popsy being unable to find the barcode on the egg box and turning it over and over and then banging it huffily down on the counter so that the omelette you were going to have for lunch starts making itself right there in the shop, and then spending the next ten minutes trying to manually type in the numbers – tutting and sighing all the time – until she eventually hits 'enter' and the display screen charges up a gross of Brussels sprout trees at £456?

It's why I've never signed up for the airport retinal identification scheme, tempting though it is. There's always some smug bugger from your plane who doesn't join the back of the immigration queue but strides airily past to the scanner, presses his eye up to the lens like Captain Kirk, and swans through to pick up his matching luggage and Louis Vuitton ski-bag while you're still rummaging through your duty-free bags for a passport.

But I just know that if I ever got around to signing up to this human barcode system I'd end up flying into Heathrow in the middle of the night, sauntering up to the machine, pressing my eye to the scanner and being told that I can't come into the country because I am four tins of skipjack tuna in brine, and did I know that if I take one more tin I get a free jar of Hellmann's?

Academic Sex

When a fruity-looking old don from a pay-as-you-go Mickey Mouse university like Buckingham writes a slobbering piece in the *Times Educational Supplement* about how 'There will be a girl in class who flashes her admiration ... enjoy her! She's a perk,' one is always, inevitably, going to feel the impulse to vomit.

I certainly felt it when I saw those pictures of Terence Kealey, Buckingham's vice-chancellor, with his great big Professor Brainstawm head, the standard-issue hair tufts above the ears, the unruly eyebrows, and read about how, 'she will flaunt you her curves, which you should admire, daily, to spice up your sex life, nightly, with your wife'.

I was sick mostly at the thought of the old goat storing up images of his students in the old fantasy-bank (schoolboys have a more satisfying, internally-rhymed name for it) and then running through them in his mind while heaving away later on top of the missus who no longer quite does it for him.

But I was also revolted by this so-called senior academic's misuse of a straightforward transitive verb. She may well 'flaunt her curves'. She may well 'flaunt them *at* you', which puts 'you' in the dative (in Latin, *tibi*) and the curves safely in the accusative, where they should be. For the object of the sentence, the noun in the accusative, must be that which is flaunted. 'Flaunt you her curves' is a solecism. A meaningless word pile. The old ram was clearly so excited with thoughts of his students' hidden bits that he lost all control of his grammar. And that is what makes him unfit for purpose. Leer, by all means. But leer with grammatical precision.

Prof Brainstawm goes on to compare the look-but-don't-touch role of the lecturer to a punter in Stringfellows, and I have to say, as a modern man, that upsets me. I don't like to hear women spoken of like that. I am a feminist. I absolutely believe in women's rights to equality in law, society and the workplace; that they should have their own running races and everything. All that. So I was sitting there, huffing and puffing about this old pant-rummager, and then I thought, 'Hang on, let's be honest about this, how different is he from me?'

In my last year at university, and for several years afterwards, I toyed with the idea of a career in academia. I got the grades, I was offered the funding, I rather enjoyed the library grind of it. But journalism distracted and only later, as the excitement of the daily newsroom slog began to pale, did I begin to think again of doing the DPhil and going back to teach.

And then I realised that my newfound academic zeal had nothing to do with tiring of journalism, and nothing to do with intellectual curiosity. I just wanted to sleep with teenage girls. That was it. That was the only reason. Plump young ladies sitting there in the tutorial, all wet-eyed and tight-skirted, bulging and blooming. Staring at you. Hungry for information. Hungry for anything you have to offer.

And the reason the urge was so potent was because I would be making up for lost time. In three years at Oxford I had sex with only five girls. Three years holed up in the middle of nowhere with 6,000 perfectly presentable (if occasionally somewhat over-serious) young women, and I managed to get it on with only five of them. It's pathetic. The greatest waste of time of my life. To this day, hardly an hour goes by when I do not get up from my desk, pace my study, and then fall to my knees, weeping, and cry aloud: 'Five, goddamit! Only five! What was I *thinking* of?'

What I was thinking of, of course, was getting a stonking degree. And I did. Right up there in the top handful for the year. And that is because I was not screwing my socks off, and so had time to read and write and think. And so they asked me to come back and teach. And I thought about it very seriously. I thought about it, on and off, for the next ten years, even as journalism started to go reasonably well for me. And it was a long time before I realised that I was considering a 'return to academia' (as failed men of letters always rather heroically call it – as if, like Han Solo in the *Millennium Falcon*, it is never too late to come swooping back into the picture and save the day), purely so I could have sex with my students.

I solved the problem in a different way, in the end, by looking up all the girls I had fancied at university and sleeping with them now, ten years later, ticking them off retrospectively (I guess we were ticking each other off) and then sort of mentally plugging them back into my past and – *pace* Stalin – rewriting my teenage sexual history.

I may have slept with only five girls at university. But I have probably slept with 12 or 15 girls who were *at university with me*. It's a nice grammatical distinction. And one that I am very well qualified to make, having, as I said, had plenty of time to work extremely hard at my English degree, what with all the shagging I wasn't doing.

And I'd guess it was the same for Dr Kealey. He'll have got where he is by first getting a great degree because he was too thin and spotty to get laid very much. And now he sits there in lectures, sick with 50 years of blue-ballitis, wishing he could turn back the clock, screw the girls, and to hell with the lifetime of pedagogy.

And I dare say it's the same for all academics. For they are all – every last one of them – people who got first-class degrees because they didn't have very much sex. And they are all very angry about it. And they become tutors and lecturers so they can go back and make up for it. It is this fascinating paradox on which the whole structure of world tertiary education rests.

And if I suggested above that I have in some way got all

this out of my system, I lied. In the last few years I have found myself invited to universities more and more, to speak at the Oxford Union, to guest-edit a student magazine, to address the Cambridge University Food Society, whatever. I have accepted these invitations only very occasionally and, now that I am married, I don't accept them at all. Because on every single occasion, I think without fail, I have copped off with the first student I met.

Sex is what universities are for. For geeks to lose their virginity and studs to get their numbers up, for gays to come out or go back in, for public schoolboys to have their eyes opened by a big-arsed lass from the Valleys and council-estate girls to grab a bit of posh; for old to do it with young, poet with critic, student with teacher, counsellor with counselled, patient with doctor, friend with friend, drunk, stoned, high as a kite or stone-cold sober, and there is no point pretending otherwise.

To Dr Kealey, I say: put up or shut up. For heaven's sake, find a girl you like, give her one from me, and then go back to your books, your lecturing, and, if she'll have you, your wife.

Lunch

I was randomly channel flicking after the News one evening, when I hit a programme where Keith Allen was going to look for Keith Floyd to talk about how they were both called Keith. A whole programme. Poised with my thumb over the channel button I hovered briefly, interested to see how Floyd, who has been hunkered down in France for the last few years, was looking.

Allen arrived at Floyd's house, walked in, through to the drawing room and ... Oh, my God! I sat up in my chair and leaned forward. I had never seen a man looking so terrible. The voiceover said he was 65. I thought they'd made a mistake. He looked 85. He was bloated and wan, his features barely discernible through the heavy make-up they'd used to hide the worst of it. He seemed to inhabit the space between Mickey Rourke's grandfather and Shane MacGowan, if Shane hadn't looked after himself so well.

He was drinking champagne and smoking a fag and making those two theoretical pleasures look as tragic as they can ever have looked.

I met Floyd only a couple of times, maybe ten years ago, and thought then that he must be seventy. But I could not understand much of what he said and, to be honest, drunkard though I am, cataclysmic booze-abuser though I have often been, alcoholism at that level makes me feel uncomfortable. All the grinning and nodding you have to do, and pretending to know what they're talking about. You know how it is.

'He can't possibly last the year,' I said aloud. 'It's a miracle he's still alive.'

It turns out he wasn't. Next day we learned that Floyd had sat down with a glass of wine to watch the programme and, by the time the opening credits rolled, he was dead. Of a heart-attack, naturally. Although he also had bowel cancer, which goes very much with the territory, and was presumably why he looked quite as bad as he did.

In the aftermath of his death, everyone went on about what a great 'luncher' he had been. Gin-flavoured tears of nostalgia welled. Just as they had when Keith Waterhouse died a couple of weeks before. So sad, to lose another bon viveur. Another man who knew the value of a fag and a glass of wine. Another man who had a 'zest for life' – the sick cliché we always use to describe men who are killed by the way they live (whether that's by drink and drugs and cigarettes or some dumb-arse dangerous sport).

The great Waterhouse was lucky enough to live out a decent term, of course, and his lunching did not prevent him creating a serious, lucrative and very possibly lasting body of work. Not so Floyd. Waterhouse was famous and beloved despite his drinking, Floyd because of it.

On the day after his death I got dozens of calls from the media asking me to comment. I said I couldn't, I didn't know the man. I don't think I ever even saw him on the telly. I was at boarding school and university during Floyd's long-ago heyday, and on the very rare occasions when life got so dull that I wanted to watch television, it certainly wasn't to listen to a drunk in a bow-tie wibbling on about something I wasn't remotely interested in. That's what I went to lectures for.

But still they wanted me to say something. If not about Floyd himself, then about his last lunch, about the joys of lunching, about the golden age of lunching. 'Come on Giles,' they seemed to be saying, 'you're a posh, sweary amateur presenter of food programmes who is frequently pissed on television ... you basically *are* Keith Floyd.'

And that gave me the heebie-jeebies. Because I don't want

to die at 65, puffy and befuddled and unfulfilled. I don't want Floyd's death and I don't want his life either. I don't want to be remembered as a greedy pisshead with a posh voice wearing a bow-tie. It's why I don't wear a bow-tie.

And that's why I am no longer a celebrant of the art of 'lunching', like all these dipso losers they wheel out whenever an alcoholic dies, to talk nostalgically about the grand old days when going to a restaurant in the middle of the working day and getting crap-faced was considered an 'art'.

Because it's not, you know. It's terribly, terribly sad. As a journalist, I caught the very end of it. I went for lunch with my boss on my first day at the *Telegraph* in 1993 and only after we'd finished the third bottle of Rioja and ordered the fourth did I summon up the courage to ask if we were going to eat anything.

And that was how the next three or four years went. I remember very little. I was drunk all the time. All the time. I slept under my desk in the afternoon. I became very fat, and very unhappy. But I had to keep lunching. To lunch 'properly' was a badge of honour that implied trustworthiness, honesty and decency. To stop after a couple of glasses was as bad as to be teetotal or to be gay or to be left-wing or to be a girl.

Oh yes, lunching wasn't for girls. When the few lunchers that are left look back on the good old days, what they're mostly remembering is a time when the only women in the office were the secretaries who held your calls while you slept it off. It was a man's world, and men who lunched had several broken marriages and a handful of scattered, resentful, barely-fathered children to show for it.

But then women came to the workplace, and they don't lunch like that. They don't live like that. And it made the men look bad. And lunching began to die out. And so did the lunchers. So many of my former bosses and colleagues. One fell down the stairs drunk after lunch, cracked his head and died. Three that I can think of heart-attacked or stroked from booze and fags. Two lost limbs. A couple of transplants. Plus the fag-related cancers. And for what? For the honour of being one of the boys. One of the lunchers.

The pressure is still there in some quarters. With my foodie boots on I could 'lunch' big and long and drunken, free, every day. I do it maybe once a month. I sit among fat, drunk men who smell of fags, bon viveurs to a man, and if I try and leave early to see my girlfriend, or stop after a couple of glasses so I can work in the afternoon, they all go 'wooooo' and make limp-wrist gestures. I'm letting down the men as badly as if I were deserting a trench at Ypres.

Inside, these men are great and talented and fun and wise, but they have fallen for the lunching myth. They have not done half the things they could have done, or been half the men they might have. They'll lose everything, they will die young and ugly, and they can't even choose where.

And the day afterwards their friends will get together and plough through a big, fatty lunch, hoon down a pack of fags, raise a giant glass of alcohol, and say, 'It's what he would have wanted.'

But it isn't. Not if he had really thought about it.

Quiz Shows

I did a TV game show recently with Sophie Dahl. Some others, too, but they're neither here nor there. All you need to know is that there was me and a supermodel, alone under lights, quite heavily made-up in front of a large audience, raring to answer the quizmaster's questions. Well, quizmistress. Okay, it was Sue Perkins. Obviously. I am not allowed on telly unless Perky Perks is there to hold my hand and keep me calm, and make sure I don't punch anyone or try to light my farts.

I make no apologies for going on a game show. I do not accept the validity of concepts such as 'selling out' and 'cheapening oneself'. Okay, so Anatole Kaletsky doesn't do TV quiz shows. But I bet the people from *Strictly* wouldn't have to ask him twice.

Doing a quiz show requires no thought, preparation or graft, it pays a lot better than this mug's game where I slog for my daily bread, and while you are expected to be halfway presentable you don't have to go so far as to iron a shirt, because they do that for you. And you get a goody-bag to take home, too, usually containing some sort of fruit cordial and an interesting chutney.

The first thing I ever did on telly was a quiz show. A *Weakest Link* 'Journalists Special' in which I slaughtered the likes of Lynn Barber, Dominic Mohan (now editor of the *Sun*), and Deirdre out of 'Dear Deirdre', to earn first place and a whopping eleven-and-a-half grand cheque. Which I then had to give to charity. All of it. Personally, I believe that if starving little fly-blown perishers from Chad want to get their hands on the best part of twelve gees then let them go on the telly themselves and be first to the buzzer on such questions as 'What "c" is the opposite of "dog"?' and 'Which "J" had the surname "Christ"?'

Determined to recoup some of that sickening financial loss, I subsequently paraded my general knowledge skills on every half-arsed digital, free-view and pay-as-you-snooze Q&A format I could, and did very nicely, thank you. The money goes in a separate bank account and only last week there was enough silted up there to buy a controlling interest in the *Observer*. Although I chose to purchase a new KitKat Chunky Caramel instead.

But this quiz show last week was the first I had done on a proper channel in ages. It's called *Huge Massive Big Food Fight*, or something, and started its run this week on Channel 4. Sue asks questions to two teams, one captained by Hugh Fearnley-Whittingstall and the other captained by some random rotating foodie (not a foodie on a potter's wheel, just, you know, a different one each week). And then each skipper gets a celeb to play with. On 'my' show the guests were Sophie Dahl and Clarissa Dickson-Wright. And which one do you think I got to sit next to and fondle and whisper sweet nothings to? Yup. Hellooooo, Clarissa.

But I did get some quality face time with Soph before the show. We'd never met, so coming down to the green room from make-up and bumping into her outside the lift I was pretty delighted to be greeted with the sort of 'hello' that suggested she knew who I was. Just think: *Times* columnist recognised by massive international megamodel and granddaughter of *Fantastic Mr Fox* creator, Roald. Stick that in yer pipe, Rifkind.

Over some posh, untouched snack food I did my best to make a favourable impression, but my hilarious lines came back from Sophie with ice on them. I didn't fret too badly. I rarely manage to make tall women laugh. They always think I'm trying to compensate for being short. When in truth I am only short to compensate for being so funny.

I tried straight chitchat, admired her lovely engagement ring, all that. Did okay, but nothing special. And then even on set, when some sort of banter is supposed to build up, I stalled again. Not a flicker from Dahl. The audience were cackling away quite happily, but then they were all quite short. And bussed in from places where it's still one telly per street.

Afterwards, a quick drink then make-up off, and there's Sophie again. One last chance. Halfway through wiping off my slap with a Wet One, I move in for a goodbye kiss. The world-famous beauty recoils like a cat dodging a bucket of water.

Is it the slimy Wet One juice glinting in my mossy beard?

Is it the smell of tuna roll on my breath?

Is it that I'm just too short?

It seems to run deeper than that.

She does allow a small kiss, eventually, and as our cheeks brush she says quietly: 'Don't ever review my poetry again!'

Her poetry? Is she mistaking me for William Hazlitt? And herself for Wordsworth? I do my baffled, 'who, me?' face (as Hazlitt would no doubt have done), and she says, 'It was the meanest thing you've ever written.'

I wrack my brains. Poetry, poetry, poetry?

Oh, GOD. Her poetry.

Seven years ago, it was announced that Sophie's first novel was to be published. Well, what the hell else was I going to write about that week? Iraq? The NHS? For Heaven's sake, supermodels writing 'novels' is what a clown like me lives for.

I was very mean. Very, very mean. I addressed my 1,000 words very much *ad feminam*, declaring, 'You've got a little bit of history with writing rude things, haven't you, Soph?' and then quoted, more or less in full, a poem she had written for an art exhibition in my local pub in 1997, when, to be fair, she was only 19.

I don't think I explicitly said the poem was bad. We post-structuralists tend not to make *a priori* value judgements like that. I merely quoted some lines in a mock-enthusiastic way – lines such as 'Little man,/Last Saturday you told me you loved me/ But then you called me Kirsty' – and then sneered like the worst kind of Regency fop, ungracious, mocking and intellectually snobby.

The thing was, I never expected to meet her. As one doesn't with supermodels. I didn't think of her as a real person. I was just a hack, hiding behind a computer screen spewing venom. I never dreamed I would one day get the chance to flaunt my arse on telly for fat pay-offs, and thus move into that glittering world where all the people I've ripped to shreds over the last ten years actually live and breathe.

It can be terrifying. Three minutes before my first appearance on *Richard and Judy*, for example, Richard put his head round the dressing-room door and reminded me of the diary piece I did at the expense of his wife in 1999. It happens more or less weekly, and it is what you have to accept if you unexpectedly creep from one world, however briefly and cravenly, into another.

Forced to confront Sophie Dahl's seven-year recall and the misery I clearly once caused a real, well-intentioned, not much more than teenage girl, I am forced to ask whether it was a very nice thing to do, whether I was just not a very nice person, and whether I have changed. And if not, am I going to change? And if I do, then what on earth am I going to write about from now on?

That, and nothing to do with spurious notions of dignity, is why a journalist shouldn't do game shows.

Ringtones

Look, bruv, I don't care what old people say, I think it's wicked that the Crazy Frog mobile telephone ringtone went straight into the charts at No 1. I mean, like, the news will probably have pop purists weeping for the days when young men and women hunkered round the old crystal set to listen to Radio Jemima, or whatever it was, broadcasting from a rusty old studio mounted on a whale in the Irish Sea, to find out whether 'Love Me Do' had been knocked off the No. 1 slot by the sound of an honest-to-goodness desktop, Bakelite, telephone bell-ring. But that's the past. And you've got to big up the kind of stuff being achieved in the modern music scene today.

It's no good sitting around talking about the 1930s, or whenever them Beatles were around, and saying: 'Aye, them were the days – when men were men, birds weren't afraid of a good snog and notification of an incoming telephonicular communication was one hundred per cent acoustic.' That's just so lame.

I mean, how different was it back then, anyway? Alan 'Titch' Freeman was probbly just saying fings like: 'Hi there, pop pickers. This week it's up, up, up, for the corridor-tastic wall-mounted telephone hammer-on-bell ring, but no movement at all for the boring old doorbell. Meanwhile, the red telephone box at the end of my road has a cut a spondoolicious deal with Polygram and its first 45 is out next week. Smashing.'

But these days fings are well more good. Personally, I fink it's a brilliant new departure for pop music, which was always going to come under pressure from the online download zippy file mpeg iPod fing anyway, wasn't it? Speaking of which, I'd love to be able to get a record of that noise my computer makes when it comes on, you know: diddle-ing-ding-diiiing!! It's wicked. I often have mates round on a Friday evening to drink a few beers, smoke some doobs and listen to it repeatedly as we switch our 'puters on and off. Except my best mate, Baz, he's got a Mac, and it makes a different noise, so he can't come.

Yes, music is wicked these days. I don't know what the old folk are talking about when they get all misty-eyed about Elvis and Donny Osmond.

I mean, could you have stored, like, about a billion songs in an Elvis record and also used it to pay the congestion charge? Exactly. 'King', my arse. The only one of Elvis's that I know is 'Tie Me Kangaroo Down, Sport', but personally I much prefer that noise that dust-carts make when they're reversing. You know: 'Meeeep . . . meeeep . . . meeeep.' It's blatantly wicked, and you can just totally trance out and stuff.

In America, dust-carts just go 'this vehicle is reversing . . . this vehicle is reversing . . . this vehicle is reversing . . .' which is just, like, totally pony, but that's coz American pop music is, like, way behind what we're doing in Britain.

Another tune that I downloaded recently is from Camden Council Traffic Solutions featuring a Couple of Blokes from Murphy. It's the sound of an angle-grinder cutting up an old speed bump which they put in last week but have decided to move. It's wicked. I usually put it on when me girl comes round for a shag. We also watch the video. The Murphy blokes have this wicked green van which they spend most of the time sitting in drinking tea.

Old people hear the news that some bleepy noise from a stupid little plastic thing which you have in your pocket for talking to your mates and taking photos of your bum to text to your nan when you is pissed has got to No. 1, and say that it is symptomatic of the ruination of music and the end of culture, but to them I say, you have to listen to it two or free times before you get into it.

And if you still don't like it, then maybe you should try something different but similar. For example, you might want to check out the No. 1 in the album charts, which is a collection of the almost inaudible little waltz-like tunes that they play down the phone for about an hour when you call the gas company to say that you can smell sumfink funny coming from the boiler and also your wife has stopped breathing.

And they say the big hit of the summer in all the clubs down Faliraki and Puerto Banús is going to be that bloke who goes 'mind the gap . . . mind the gap . . .' down the Underground.

Or perhaps what will light your fire is a new compilation from Mercedes-Benz which contains no fewer than 23 different car alarms going off in suburban streets at the crack of dawn on a Sunday simply because a sparrow has shat on the hood from the branches of an overhanging tree.

Hang on, I think the bloke downstairs has got his iPod speakers on full blast to play the new hit single from Tops Pizza in Tufnell Park, which is the sound of a teenager on £1 an hour screeching a moped with a hole in the exhaust up my road at four in the morning to deliver a Hawaiian with extra pineapple to the stoneheads at No. 46.

Can you hear it? It's well wicked, it goes: 'waaaaaaaaa Glonk waaaaaaaaa Glonk waaaaaaaaaaa Glonk . . .' The Glonk is the sound of him hitting the speed bumps which the council are coming round tomorrow with the Murphy boys to move.

No wait, I tell a lie, he hasn't got his iPod speakers on at all. It's the actual bloke from Tops Pizza coming down the roads on his moped.

Wicked! I love live music.

Census 2011

The 2011 Census, forward to which I can hardly wait, will ask us for the first time how much we earn and how we earn it. Time was you didn't talk about that sort of thing in public. Time still is, in fact. I certainly won't be filling that bit in. Other journalists might find out what I'm paid and be jealous.

Mind you, I won't be filling in any of it. I never have filled in a census. Never will. When it comes to putting words down on a piece of paper my rule is three pounds a word, or forget it. Oops, bugger, the cat's out of the bag.

I didn't complete the 1991 Census, I remember, because my student housemates and I were in dispute with the local authority about whether we actually lived in our house or even, technically, existed at all. We argued that we did not live there, and were thus exempt from paying the poll tax. As a result we had a 'never acknowledge the post' rule, unless thanking mater and pater for a hamper or the cheque they had sent to cover our car insurance.

In 2001 I didn't fill it in because I had read that the penalty for census evasion was a jail term – I was struggling with my first novel at the time, and thought chokey would be the ideal place to get away from the competing demands on my attention. I lay awake for weeks with my bags packed, waiting for the rozzers, but they never came. I might as well have filled it in. In the 'religion' section I could have put 'Jedi' – apparently that was a great hoot. I would probably still be chuckling about it now.

And I will not be filling in the 2011 Census because as well as enshrining the vulgarity and greed of our money-obsessed culture, the new Census will reflect other changes to society which depress me to hell. For example, it will be made shorter and less complicated to allow for dwindling intellects and attention spans (why not just shoot the thick people and ask the rest of us whatever you want?). Furthermore, technology and leisure will feature heavily, as well as questions about sex, which fair sends a shiver down my spine.

Worried about all this, I called the Census Office to ask if they might send me a sneak preview. They said they had only a rough working document and I attach it here:

The Census: 2011 (provisional draft)
1. All right?
2. How much do you earn?
3. What about your mates?
4. What about your doris?
5. Don't you hate it when a bird earns more than you do?
6. Can you believe what that Wayne Rooney's on a week?
7. If you could have any car in the whole wide world, would you get a Ferrari or an Aston Martin or one of them 4x4s?
8. What would you do if you won the Lottery?
9. Or *Who Wants to Be a Millionaire?*
10. Or what about if someone died and left you a million paand?
11. Would you consider murdering someone for their money?
12. Not even for a million paand?
13. Would you let your doris shag another man for a million paand?
14. Have you ever thought of getting up off your fat arse and actually earning some money?
15. How many televisions have you got in your house?
16. How many have you got in your car?
17. How many have you got in your phone?

18. How many hours a day do you spend on the Internet?
19. And is that mostly just looking at porn?
20. Do you shag a lot?
21. How big is your knob?
22. If you ever end up in a persistent vegetative state, thereby costing the government £1,500 a day to keep you alive (which over two years is more than a million paand), do we have permission to stop feeding you until you die?
23. What if you're only a bit vegetative?
24. What about if you're just old and annoying?
25. How good-looking are you?
26. What about her indoors?
27. Do you think Beyoncé is fit, or what?
28. Do you think if your doris is a bit of a minger you should be allowed to shag other birds because you're a bloke and it's what you're basically programmed to do?
29. Are you a woofter?
30. Which football team do you support?
31. What do you mean 'not interested in football'? You *are* a woofter. Everyone's interested in football. Put a team down. This question is not optional.
32. Look, just write 'Manchester United'.
33. What newspaper do you read? (If you refuse to answer this question on the grounds that it is an infringement of your freedom of thought and that the information may be used against you by the American government, then we'll know you read *The Guardian* anyway, and are thus probably a woofter.)

Processed Ham

In the aftermath of 'Watergate', as I think we can properly call the recent scandal about liquid bulking agents in processed ham (although the name does sound strangely familiar), percentages of relative meat content were published in the media for such things as Turkey Twizzlers, Ye Olde Oak ham and Matteson's 'Thomas-Shaped' Ham Slices (what shape is Thomas, for the Lord's sake? Thomas who? Thomas More? Doubting Thomas? My John Thomas? Oh God . . . it's Thomas the Tank Engine, isn't it?).

On average, it transpired, the mass was made up of between 14 and 66 per cent water. Some, in other words, were little more than puddles through which battery-farmed livestock had trotted on the way to the abattoir.

I have not eaten such stuff in years. I do not believe that the words 'Bernard', 'Matthews', 'wafer', 'thin', 'turkey', and 'ham' can rationally be accommodated in the same short sentence (although it comes as no surprise to hear that when they do it is to describe something that is only 60 per cent 'meat').

The sad fact is that every new food horror story is based on stuff I have known for years, and on the basis of which I have already eliminated it from my diet. That's why I eat almost nothing. In the quest to avoid cancer, obesity, heart disease, hyperactivity, liver and kidney failure, salmonella, listeria, botulism, erectile dysfunction, halitosis, illiteracy and Ebola I am down to a diet of acorns, paving stones and moss with occasional tiny yoghurt drinks (which give you dysentery anyway).

Most of the products implicated in the story were 'reformed' meats, created through a process by which the last and unholiest remnants of very poorly husbanded animals are mechanically reclaimed from the already ransacked corpse and then mashed with additives and water and squeezed and cut (with the sort of machines children use on Plasticine) into meat-slice imitations whose exact dimensions are determined at marketing meetings by men in short-sleeved shirts with polyester ties, sweaty armpits and a company Rover.

You know how they make those bits of ham stick together in sliceable squares so you can fold them into your sandwiches? They do it with hydrocolloids such as carrageenan and sodium alginate that were originally developed for the production of tinned dog food. You remember those ads? The ones where the cylinder of glistening brown donkey-meat is sliced so that one half falls on to its back with a satisfying thud as the voice says, 'Top breeders recommend it because it's solid nourishment'? It was solid because of hydrocolloids.

If, God help you, you make a habit of eating that crap, then of all the ingredients, the water in it is the least of your problems.

Vintage Children's Television

The first time I was sent by a newspaper to watch an animated kiddies' film, the paper was the *Mail on Sunday*, the film was *Toy Story 2* and the screening was in New York. The *Mail* had missed the boat on the London pre-screenings and so, because money is no object there, I was handed a 24-hour club-class return and a disposable toothbrush and sent to review the film stateside. Things did not work out, journalistically.

Uncaged for a day from the office grind, I met up with an old friend at the then trendy Whiskey Bar at the Paramount, picked up some lady friends of his from work at Condé Nast and headed downtown to his drug dealer's East Village loft apartment to pick up some bits and pieces to get us through the night.

Nine hours later we were still there and I had missed the city's last showing of the film. On the plus side, my nosebleed had stopped and I was engaged to a Chinese-American girl who worked in the beauty department at *Vogue*. At least, I think she was a girl.

At 5 a.m. the dealer threw us out and we went to a pool hall where I picked a fight over the pronunciation of 'merlot' and a man restarted my nosebleed for me. At 10, I was held over by airport officials who didn't want to let me on the plane with blood in my moustache and by lunchtime I was on the following flight, snoozing merrily thanks to a strip of Xanax and three Martell miniatures with soda. I woke an hour before landing, copied a review out of *Time* magazine and parted company with the *Mail* soon afterwards.

And all because drugs are bad. Bad, bad, bad. Which is

why it was so odd to find myself sitting in a screening room in Soho several years later, the week they launched the movie of *The Magic Roundabout*, with a bunch of journalists laughing riotously at all the drug references.

At one point, staring into a river of volcanic lava, Dylan, the hippy rabbit, drools: 'Mmm, hot rocks . . .' Ye gods, a crack reference in a movie for children. Not just a cheeky marijuana gag, but a Class A drug joke dropped casually into a children's movie just to keep the parents entertained. It happens a lot in the film (the old grass/grass double entendre gets a thorough workout) and is enough to make a terrible prude of a man who was born in time to see six months of the 1960s, but has had just about enough of this 'wasn't kids' TV trippy in the old days?' crap.

In *Sprung! The Magic Roundabout*, Dougal's sugar addiction is played out as if it were a smack problem, to huge audience laughs. The sad thing is that the sugar lumps need no longer stand as a metaphor for something, since we now know that excessive sugar consumption represents as big a threat to our children as any narcotic does.

If it's not Dougal's sugar or Ermintrude's flowers then it's the blue string soup in the Clangers, Paddington's marmalade, Madame Cholet's bramble pudding, Black Beauty's hay . . . Is it meant to be funny in some way that they might be on drugs?

It was the drugs, presumably, that made them such inveterate shaggers. One thinks of all the nonsense about Pugwash and Master Bates (none of it true), the one about the porn mag in *Rupert the Bear*, and Roobarb and Custard supposedly enjoying a spot of coitus in ano during the credits. It's all rubbish, and it is all designed to hide the truth that children's television in the 1970s was a lot of plotless drivel written by public school dropouts who knew the right people.

Don't come to me with your Fingerbobs and your Flumps and your Jamie and the Magic bleeding Torch. They weren't on drugs. The creative wonks behind them barely had minds to be out of.

This is evidenced quite neatly by the attempt to breathe CGI life into the pastel prattery of *The Magic Roundabout*. For all its high-resolution pastiche psychedelia, the film is as dreary as a pigeon. The charm of Ivor Wood's stop-frame animation, such as it was, derived from the wheels and springs that gave each character its motive force. To reanimate them with the almost-vitality of *Toy Story* is terribly dislocating when you have known them as clomping puppets.

I don't want to see Florence as ersatz flesh-and-blood, voiced by Kylie Minogue and appearing to die (death, in *The Magic Roundabout*!). I don't want to see Dougal's hairs move individually, for Christ's sake, he's a bog brush on casters.

Because those five-minute pre-news wonders never had linear plots, the film-makers have had to create a negative Zebedee (called ZeeBadDee) so as to generate the kind of transparent moral polarity that junior culture requires in the 21st century. But in the end it is just an hour-long chase sequence decorated with clichés borrowed from *Raiders of the Lost Ark* and *The Lord of the Rings*.

Plotlessness in the original was forgiven because we knew it was Emma Thompson's dad writing random scripts over a French soundtrack he could not understand. But that doesn't mean it was good.

It began in the mid-1990s, this patronising reverence for the television of the 1970s, and it happened because we felt guilty about getting so mercenary and pseudo-sophisticated in the 1980s. With the death of Thatcherism, a whole generation decided that the antediluvian naivety of its youth had been cool. The amateurism and cheapness of the programming was mistaken for 'trippiness' and wild creativity.

And so film-makers have been remaking the culture over and over in the image of their own youth – not just the children's programmes but the adult rubbish, too. *Starsky and Hutch*, *Charlie's Angels*, even *The A-Team*, have been made into full-length features. It cannot be long before they do it with *CHiPs*, *Blake's Seven* and *The Amazing Adventures of Morph*.

When they do, you'll find me on the floor of a loft apartment somewhere, with pin-prick pupils and just the very beginnings of a nosebleed.

Smacking and Smoking

There was a worrying pile-up in the legislative process quite recently, as smoking in public and a parent's right to smack came under parliamentary scrutiny in the same week. Or was it about smacking in public and a parent's right to smoke? I forget. Suddenly I see a group of freezing secretaries huddled outside the revolving doors of the office on a snowy morning, whacking the bejesus out of a four-year-old before returning miserably to their soulless little no-smacking work stations. (And then there is the even more surreal image of a stern father cramming a toddler into his Meerschaum and declaring, as he tamps it down with a yellow thumb and puts a Swan Vesta to its curly locks: 'He's my son, and I'll damn well smoke him if I want to . . .')

In the cases of both smacking and smoking, the issue is not whether or not they are wrong, but whether legislation is required to prevent them. Can we decide for ourselves, or should it be left to the nanny state? And should Nanny State be allowed to smack us, or should she just lock us in our bedroom until Father gets home?

The danger that becomes apparent, though, as these two great issues come under consideration, is the possibility that they might one day legislate against one without the other. Because this would be a disaster.

And I'll tell you for why. Between 80 and 90 per cent of parents who smack are smokers.* And more than 90 per cent of smokers smack.** This is because a chap whose impatient and short-tempered disposition leads him to give his kid a smart whack on the backside rather than explain why widdling into the toaster is wrong, is the same chap who, when confronted with a testing or infuriating or boring situation which is not the fault of a nearby child, will, rather than look for a solution, simply light a fag. Experience tells this fellow: if the kid gets into trouble, whack it. If you get into trouble, smoke. It's a clear moral code.

The saving grace of this, admittedly barbaric, modus vivendi is that the children of such parents are invariably corrected with a weedy whack of the weaker left hand, because the right hand always has a fag in it.

So you see, a law that forces a man to give up his 60 Rothmans a day without accompanying legislation against whacking his kids will create not only a father with a free right hand, but a father constantly irritable because he is not allowed to smoke. It will be carnage. Take away the fags and you increase the brutality of the smacking, remove the right to smack and watch the poor, desperate parents smoke themselves into a coma. It's positively Newtonian in its simplicity.

Whether or not legislative coercion is the key to reinforcing social responsibility, I don't know. I'm not Simon Jenkins. I tend to take a liberal paternalist view of these things, but you wouldn't know that. Because telling you what I believe is not my job. I'm a professional silly-arse. What I'm supposed to write is that it's daft trying to use the law to make us better people, because that's what most other laws are for, and nobody pays any attention to them. Except for the laws of cricket.

And the law of the jungle. And the offside law. And Jude Law.

But the fact remains that hitting children and smoking fags are grim and uncivilised activities. But it is not the doing of them ourselves that is wrong, it is the doing of them by other people that is so reprehensible. This is true of almost everything. Thus, if we are to ban smoking in public and smacking children, we must also pass laws to prohibit:

Chewing gum.

Wearing tattoos.

Eating in public.

Speaking in interrogative half-statements that rise to an implied question mark?

Wearing clothes that show your midriff, if you are at or past the point of podginess which makes your tummy button look like a wry smile.

Doing that horrid, jerky, aggressive walk that skinny young Englishmen do with their feet pointing to ten-to-two and their knees not really bending.

Or the other horrid walk, with the shoulders rolling and eyes darting from left to right to see if anyone wants a fight.

And we'd need a law against not walking on escalators (because if the guy who invented the escalator had wanted to invent a thing you just stand still on to move upwards he would have invented the lift).

And against checking your balance and printing a mini-statement and ordering a chequebook before withdrawing a tenner when there are 38 people queueing behind you at a cashpoint.

And wearing shoes that display your toes if your nails are yellow or cracked, or any of them have black or blue bits. And toe rings, now I think of it. And holding a toddler to let it pee into the gutter out of its horrid little squitty toddler penis. And then congratulating it.

And then of course you'd want laws against people who have never been to a football match watching games in the pub rather than at home 'for the atmosphere'.

And against sending text messages while walking down the street and just bloody stopping dead suddenly on the pavement to do a bit of tricky punctuation. And against tutting when this happens in front of you. And tutting generally. And . . .

God, I'm furious. I need a fag.

---

* This figure is made up.

** So is this one.

Journalism

As part of its response to the criticisms of the Hutton report, and by way of apologising for the schoolboy errors of the Gilligan affair, the BBC announced plans to set up a college of journalism. Not only that, all 7,000 journalists currently working for the BBC would have to attend courses 'covering everything from practical skills such as note-taking to ethics'.

Clap, clap, clap. Just what we need. Another school. As if doing history O level means you can remember who died in the White Ship disaster, or elementary maths has left you able to say for sure whether or not two is a prime number.

You don't go to school to learn. You go to school to get drunk, copy your homework off other people and bunk off. Same as you go into journalism. This plan of the BBC's only reinforces that suspicion one has, as a child, that school exists merely as a punishment. But what possible good can this punishment do for grown hacks?

It'll just be Mark Mardell giving James Naughtie Chinese burns in the back row while John Humphrys passes round naked cartoons of Fiona Bruce, and Nicholas Witchell wedgies Matthew Amroliwala to impress Emily Maitlis. Huw Edwards will go home early in tears because Moira Stuart called him 'fatty', George Alagiah will devote his attention to bending his ruler back as far as it will go and muttering 'shatterproof, we'll soon see if it's shatterproof', and, for the whole of July, Broadcasting House will throb to the tune of 'one more week of school, one more week of sorrow, one more week in this old dump and we'll be out tomorrow'.

But if it really does want to set up this college, and it is looking for a principal (as I have read), then it could do a lot worse than appoint me, veteran that I am of the *Daily Telegraph*, *The Times*, the *Mail on Sunday*, *The Independent* and *Tatler*, and thus possessor of hard experience of the internal workings of the empires of Rupert Murdoch, Conrad Black, the Harmsworths, Condé Nast and whichever sorry old bum owned *The Independent* that year.

I never needed no skool to learn how to be a journalist, but I'd be happy to turn teacher anyway and I would begin, of course, by explaining to my pupils the First Rule of Journalism.

The First Rule of Journalism is that everything is the First Rule of Journalism.

Every single piece of advice I have ever been given in my 17 years in the business has been described as the First Rule of Journalism. This is because journalists are too drunk, too lazy and too short of attention span ever to get to the second rule.

The first First Rule of Journalism I was told was: 'Never resign, wait to be fired.' This is because, from the very outset of his career, the dream of every journalist is to survive entirely on redundancy payments.

Later, in my first month on the Street, a 'teach yourself shorthand' book was plucked from my hands, and I was told: 'First Rule of Journalism – never learn shorthand, that's what girls are for.' This was a mild variation on the already drummed-in 'First Rule of Journalism – don't learn to type. And if you can type already don't brag about it or you'll end up doing everybody's typing.' As a result, I still pretend I can't type, even though I work at home and there's nobody here but me.

And so we come to the First Rule of Journalism. This I learnt when I tried to make two separate points in a 700-word feature article in the spring of 1994. 'Giles, Giles, Giles,' said the features editor when he had read it. 'A 700-word piece is a one-point piece. Make your point in the first paragraph. Make it again in the second. Make it twice more in the middle and then conclude by making it again.'

'What if it's a 1,200-word piece?' I asked. 'That's a one-point piece, too,' he said. You will notice that I am now such a good journalist that I never make any points at all.

When I eventually started to be sent out of the office on 'stories', I soon discovered that the First Rule of Journalism is 'don't take a photographer'. If you take a photographer with you, then 43-year-old investment banker Geoffrey Mulcane, who rides a horse to work, has two wives, once played ice hockey for Albania and is exactly the case study your editor asked for, has to actually exist.

Of course, the First Rule of Journalism is 'never write anything that could get you sued'. This you achieve by applying the First Rule of Journalism, which is 'check all your facts, then double-check them, and keep all your notebooks for five years, or possibly seven'.

However, when I became editor of *The Times* Diary in 2000, I achieved the unique accolade of never receiving so much as a Christmas card from a single solicitor by a far more ingenious method than boring old fact-checking. I avoided 'stories' altogether. Instead I just wrote down funny things that (I pretended) had happened to me on the way to work, and sometimes I set word puzzles. It was a whole year before I was fired.

Jeremy Paxman and his chums don't need to be put in shorts and caps and packed off on the school bus with their protractors and set squares and Dairylea Lunchables.

They just need to remember the First Rule of Journalism, which is 'remember, it's only journalism'.

And now, if you'll excuse me, children, I have to go down the road to the secretarial college and find someone to type this out for me.

History

After centuries of doubt and uncertainty, Channel 4 has finally decided which was the worst century in the whole wide world, ever. I bet you didn't even know that it was Channel 4 which decided these things. I bet you thought that it was traditionally the job of the House of Lords but was now being decided in Brussels by faceless bureaucrats in their time off from banana-straightening duties. I'll wager that was why you were planning to vote 'No' if there was a referendum on Europe – because you didn't want Glenys Kinnock and Jacques Tati and Seve Ballesteros telling you which bleeding century was bad and which wasn't; we buy our centuries in pounds and ounces, damn and blast it, and we won't be told by some frilly-shirted, onion-smelling Frog . . .

And then it turns out it is Channel 4 that makes the decisions about which are the best and worst arbitrarily numbered sequences of 36,525 days ever. And it seems that its goggle-boffins have decided that, what with the Hundred Years War, the Black Death and the Peasants' Revolt, this week's highest new entry, and brand-new No. 1, knocking the extremely chilly 91st century BC into second spot, and the relatively nice 12th century into third, is . . . if I can just get this open . . . the 14th century!

Yaaaaayy! And also Boooooo! Down wiv curly shoes and silly cloth hats and boiled weasel with sprouts and horrid rhyming poems about knights.

Yes, indeed. We have declared a pox on the 14th century or, as even *The Times* called it last week, in case any thick people were reading, 'the 1300s'. Why do we have to call it that, now? Just who, pray tell, has not yet grasped that the number before the 'th' in centuries is always one higher than the number with which the individual dates in that century begin?

It is not hard, people. And it is time you got used to it. Because I am afraid that the rest of us, who read whole big books about the olden days with no pictures in, cannot spare the word '1300s' because we need it to describe the decade from 1300 to 1309. If we let it be used as a special-needs version of '14th century' for morons, then we're buggered when it comes to debating, say, the fluctuation of wool prices between 1301 and 1308.

Anyway, the lefty pornographers at Channel Phwoaarr plan to prove their hypothesis in a series of 'documentaries' called *World's Worst Century*. It is just stupid.

The Hundred Years War wasn't necessarily bad. Not if you were, say, an arrow maker. And it was a blessing for spread-betting companies too, which set the spread for the duration of the fight against the French at 26–31 years (in 1337), watched everyone bet short, and cleaned up for generations. And why so down on the Black Death? It was a much-needed fillip for, among other people, the wheelie-deathcart-makers (who, until 1348, had been having to give away a free bell with every cart just to get punters into the showroom). And the Peasants' Revolt was just the ticket if you were a peasant. Even if we now know that Wat Tyler only started it because he was fed up with being mistaken for a roofing magazine.

I don't see how the age of Chaucer, the century of chivalry and courtly love, of the dashing young Richard II, the birth of modern English and the last century before the arrival of cigarettes, chips, the Inquisition and Americans, can be seen as anything but the very best of all possible centuries.

It should not be left to the whim of the documentary-makers to determine how good or bad centuries are. The only way is to make a reality show, instead of a boring history series, and then let people text in their favourite centuries until only one is left.

I would like to have all the centuries locked up in a prefabricated house with hidden cameras, and let them stew. Would the apparently strait-laced 19th century (whose seedy *fin-de-siècle* side comes out when it is drunk) succumb to the saucy moves of the sexy but syphilitic 18th century? Would the moody Dark Ages lighten up when the always-game-for-a-laugh Elizabethan era took its knickers off in the pool? And what about that boozy, violent bastard, the 9th century? It is always splashing its Danegeld everywhere and slaughtering monks; surely there would be some sort of ugly clash with the dour, puritanical, mean old 17th, perhaps involving the theft of some fags?

It would have been more fun still to put them in a kitchen and let Gordon Ramsay decide. With the 650,012th century BC doing its famous pterodactyl ravioli *façon tyrannosaure* and the 23rd century cooking nothing at all because the whole world is underwater, which would Gordon choose as the best 'century chef' of all? And will the 16th century, offended by all the swearing, burn him as a witch?

No wait, better still. Since, I assume, *World's Worst Century* is being made by the same team that made *World's Worst Drivers*, then why not a *Police Stop!* meets *Time Team* car-crash series? See the carnage as the late 11th century refuses to drive on the wrong side of the road after the Norman Conquest! Watch the 15th lose a plod car in a Portsmouth housing estate because it is too young to drive! Recoil in horror as the 19th century piles its uninsured Lexus into the chap with a flag he has hired to walk in front of him!

Up with telly! Down with history!

Women

The passing of the Gender Recognition Bill allowed men to change their sex by deed poll rather than by 'surgical realignment' and simply declare themselves to be women. This means that they can compete in sporting events to great physical advantage without losing their loveliest bits and pieces to the shrill blade of the surgeon's axe (women will be allowed to do the same, not because there's any point, but because, like younger siblings, anything we do they have to be allowed to do too).

Now, this strikes me as a great thing. Not because I have any interest in winning sports competitions ('Hi, I'm Giles Coren, ladies' triple-jump champion of Poland') but because of all the other benefits such a change would bring. If I declare myself to be a woman in 2004 (becoming, perhaps, the lovely Gilella) I will be able to:

1. Sit with my back to the wall in restaurants and look at the room (do women even know that restaurants have walls?).
2. Insist on paying the bill, safe in the knowledge that I won't have to.
3. Give up in the middle of every game of chess I appear to be losing, saying: 'I don't understand why you're so competitive.'
4. Borrow a man's coat when the weather turns cold and I've come out in only a flimsy little dress because I didn't have the wit to watch the weather forecast.
5. Have casual sex when drunk without fear of embarrassing performance failures.

6. Tell the difference between *Gossip Girl* and *Hannah Montana*.
7. Have my pubic hair shaped.
8. Write a column about being a mum (or about not being a mum).
9. Prove that I'm not a virgin.
10. Stop drinking after my third pint without being called a poof.
11. Flick through glossy magazines while sitting under a hairdryer.
12. Be shrill and defensive about not having a proper job ('doing nothing all day is a full-time job, actually, and the government ought to be paying people like me to do it – if I was doing nothing all day in a major company, I'd be earning £275,000 a year').
13. Go to the loo without taking something to read.
14. Perpetuate the great 'childbirth is painful' myth to make all men feel bad simply for being alive.
15. Declare proudly that I can't cook as if it makes me some sort of latter-day Boadicea.
16. Get a sports column in a national newspaper despite knowing nothing about sport.
17. Claim I am pregnant whenever I get arrested.
18. Walk down a beach positively brimming with flat round stones without stopping to pick up a couple and skim them across the water.
19. Tell you exactly how many calories there are in a skinless, boneless breast of chicken.
20. Read Helen Fielding.
21. Read the *Daily Mail*.
22. Read your palm.
23. Interrupt stories being told by my partner to say 'The helicopter wasn't red, so much as a sort of deep maroon colour.'

24. Vote Lib Dem.
25. Watch *Escape to Victory* and not cry when Pele scores that bicycle kick to bring the POWs level with the Gestapo at 4-4.
26. Make daft generalisations about the opposite sex without people thinking I'm sexist.

Estate Agents

The National Association of Estate Agents has at last instituted a serious professional qualification for its members, with a short course followed by a proper examination.

Interviewed on the *Today* programme, the NAEA president, Melfyn Williams, was cock-a-hoop about the new 'Technical Awards' (one for residential sales and the other for residential lettings), declaring: 'I have a dream that one day all estate agents will be able to walk down the streets and hold their heads high; a dream that one day all estate agents will have passed minimum standards in the industry; and a dream that this day will go down in agency history as the day that was the catalyst for licensing in the industry.'

With rhetoric like that, it cannot fail. A new dawn may truly be upon us in which estate agents are thought of as educated men and qualified professionals, just like, for example, journalists.

But have you got what it takes to be an estate agent? Could you pass the exam and change careers to that dream job at Winkworth? Below, I reproduce some of the questions from the exam so that you can test yourself. Do well, and this may be the last Saturday morning for some time that you spend lying in bed with the papers instead of showing a lugubrious old man round a selection of scabrous bedsits in Swansea.

> **You have two hours. Please use both sides of the paper. If you need more paper, just raise your hand. Remember to read the question carefully. Cheating is fine.**
>
> **You may begin.**

Maths

1. Using either quadratic equations or a parabolic graph, explain how your 2 per cent of the £100,000 sale price comes to exactly £17,000. Do not show your workings.
2. Using trigonometry and circle theorems, show how a space 3 feet by 2 feet can be called 'a bedroom'.
3. Beginning with an 'asking price' of £699,000, show how, once you have waived your agent's fee, knocked the vendor down to account for necessary improvements and 'done a deal' on the stamp duty, your purchasing client will, if he commits himself this afternoon, be 'in and out' for 'a shade over £698,000'. (You may use a calculator for this, but do not let the client see what you are tapping in until the numbers on the screen correspond to the correct answer.)

Physics

According to Newtonian physics: 'What goes up must . . .'
a. 'Come down'; or
b. 'Carry on going up – that's the way the housing market works, luv.'

Geography

For the benefit of a prospective client, indicate the whereabouts of Ickenham, Beaconsfield and Chalfont St Giles on the attached map of London's fashionable Notting Hill Gate.

History

1. 'Henry Bolingbroke was a good king but a poor property developer.' Discuss.
2. In 1478 Richard III murdered the young princes in the Tower of London. Were the Tower of London to come on to the open market, how would you use this fact to

crank the price up with Japanese developers? And how would you stay off the subject of planning permission?

3. How might a need for extensive off-street parking have affected the aspirations of Capability Brown?

English Language

1. Write an essay entitled: 'What I diddled in the holidays.'
2. Write a piece of short fiction entitled: 'Don't worry, mate, there isn't going to be a collapse in property prices; in fact, prices are predicted to rise by 28 per cent next week in this very street, so I'd pay the asking price now before it goes up. I'm only telling you this because I like you.'
3. A synonym is a word which means the same as another word. If *loggia* is a synonym for Portaloo, and original oak floors is synonymous with wood-tiles-on-a-roll, suggest synonyms for the following: overpriced, ugly, derelict, vile, horrid, bad, black. (The examiners will be looking here for: competitive, beautiful, original, lovely, nice, good and white.)

English Literature

Shakespeare's sonnet 'When to the sessions of sweet, silent thought' uses many fiscal metaphors such as 'summon up remembrance of things past' and 'tell o'er the sad account of fore-bemoaned moan'. In your own words, use a lot of flowery language to disguise the grim truth that you are about to sell someone a property that will bankrupt him by the end of the year.

French

1. '*La plume de ma tante est plus petite que le jardin de mon oncle.*' But could your uncle improve the value of the property by giving some of this enormous garden of his over to a swimming pool?

2. Translate the following passage into French. 'This is Dollis Hill, like in the Hugh Grant movie. It's where Madonna lives. Yes, I know the people look a bit poor and scruffy and foreign, but that's your boho chic, Pierre.'

Religious Studies

1. Imagine your client has foolishly built his house on the sand. How would you persuade possible purchasers that there is no need for a full survey?

2. Christ said: 'In my father's house are many mansions . . .' Do you think there really were? Or was Jesus talking it up for a quickie sale to get round inheritance tax?

3. Moses led the Israelites in the wilderness for 40 years looking for the land of Canaan, but died without seeing it. With this in mind, write an essay entitled 'Location, location, location'.

GQ

QUESTION: What do David Blaine, BBC3, Arsenal, cocaine, Christina Aguilera, and I, your obedient servant, have in common?

ANSWER: We were all included in a list of 'The Fifty Worst Things in the World' in *GQ*.

As those of you who are between 39 and 45, are still virgins, dress at Hackett, drink imported lager straight from the bottle, and intend to fit a rear spoiler to your family saloon as soon as you get a Sunday off will already know, *GQ* is a men's magazine. The rest of you should try to imagine an in-flight duty-free catalogue for middle-aged paedophiles en route to an exhibition of mobile phone holsters in Düsseldorf.

The words are mostly in list form because there is nobody on staff who can write whole sentences with, like, punctuation and subordinate clauses and everyfink, and anyway preliterate audiences prefer loose nouns without sequence or qualification – think of all those surveys of 100 greatest people/books/congenital diseases of the domestic aardvark that get made into television series.

Most importantly, lists of 'cool stuff' offer a seamless opportunity for product placement which weary cynics like me can't help but associate with freebies for the lads. How else could 'The 100 Best Things in the World Right Now' include such tragic tat as a 'Stirling Moss racing bracelet', a 'Hogan Rider weekend bag' (I'm not making these up), '*The World at War* DVD boxset' and the Splendido at Portofino (that rest home for gin-bloated, impotent old Eurosoaks and their inflatable teenage mistresses)? I'd rather take my chance on Brucie's conveyor belt.

Once you have descended into list journalism (see also *Tatler*'s '200 Posh Kids You Might Want to Shag', and *Vogue*'s '150 Awful Tossers Who Go to a Lot of Parties'), it is hard to kick the habit. So when you've done your 100 toppest wossnames, you whack out a nice list of 'The Fifty Worst Fings in the Whole Wide Entire Weld, Innit' to fill another page and settle a few old scores. Here you pillory celebs who have been difficult about pictures, PRs who have failed to provide free cars, restaurateurs who have not been generous enough with tables . . .

But how did I, a bona fide nobody, become the latest victim of the media's obsessive list-making? What did I do to chart at No. 10, only three spots behind Lee Bowyer and 16 places ahead of 'flat chests'?

It is true that in a piece for *The Times* a few months previously I reported rumours that the British Style Awards was a Condé Nast fit-up and observed that *GQ*'s editor 'shuffled up and down the steps all night like Fred Astaire dressed for a come-as-Elvis Costello party'. But I meant that as a good thing. Nobody shuffled like Fred. And almost everyone who is anyone these days goes to parties as Elvis Costello.

I suppose I did have a public go at them for airbrushing the sensationally voluptuous Kate Winslet into an anorexic crack whore because they are terrified of ladies' wobbly bits – but so did everyone else. And if I described the magazine as a 'fantasy frottage aid for hairless prep school boys who can't reach the top shelf', it was only to help my cloistered readers build a picture.

Whatever it was that upset them, *GQ*'s response was to whack me in the 'worst' list and comment: 'His snide and irritating column is one reason to cancel your subscription to *The Times*. We have.' Sorry, but a threat to cancel your subscription? Lads, lads. That is the celebrated last resort of retired Air Chief Marshal Reginald Wibblingstock, DFSA, GhK, SNORGS (third class), of Cheesington, nr Fordingbridge, Hants. What are you doing now that you've cancelled, going back to the *Daily Telegraph*? Telling all your friends down the Conservative Association to cancel, too? Writing to your MP in green ink?

No, as it happens, you are not. Because I came into your building on Tuesday and spoke to the two old boys on reception at Vogue House (I notice your place of work is not called *GQ* House), and they tell me that you are still receiving your *Times*, same as always. So don't tell big porky whoppers.

You are still buying the paper for the sport, wot you understand, and also the telly listings. You just don't cut my column out any more and post it to your mummies with the funny bits underlined.

I should point out that a few days after this piece was published, the editor of *GQ*, Dylan Jones, got in touch with me. We ate lunch, patched up our little tiff, and I began writing a column for him, some of which appear in this very book.

Anger: managed.

(I should also point out, before you do, the irony of my having written that line about how, 'preliterate audiences prefer loose nouns without sequence or qualification – think of all those surveys of 100 greatest people/books/congenital diseases of the domestic aardvark that get made into television series' and then gone on to present, for Channel 5, such immortal clip shows as '50 Best Disaster Movies of All Time', '50 Best Comedy Movies', '50 Best Romantic Movies', etc., etc., etc.)

Formula One

NNNNNNNNNNNNGGGG WAAAOOOWWWW! What's that I hear? Surely not the sound of that never-ending procession of witless machismo, vulgarity, dumb consumerism and Eurotrashery that is Formula One racing?

Lawks, I hate Formula One. Mostly because it perpetuates the laughable, though murderous myth that driving is something that some men do better than others. But safety records show that the only people who do it really well are women between the ages of 50 and 60. And yet you don't see policemen pulling speeders over and saying: 'Who do we think we are, sir, Mrs Pepperpot?'

And it is not as if the cars are all that fast. There are myriad stupid rules restricting the power of the engines and the road-gripping force developed by aerodynamic innovation and all that. It's a whole season of flame-proofed tarmac shaggers haring around in deliberately dodgy motors.

But why stop there? Why not follow the example of Formula Minicab and insist that cars are driven only in third gear, have pirate radio playing one notch below comfortably audible and smell of fish curry? Why not make like Formula Old Dear and give them 40-year-old cars in which they can only just see over the steering wheel, and make them drive three miles down a windy lane to the village shop without hitting a horse?

All I know is that if I get stopped for bad driving in my Ford Fiesta by some Formula One-loving copper I will have him in the palm of my hand when I explain that, far from being a dangerous old nail, my car conforms to the rigorous demands of Formula Giley, which insist that headlamps be no brighter than a fridge light, exhaust pipes must have two punctures and be attached to the chassis only by rust, brake pads thicker than a slice of prosciutto are forbidden and, as of this season, tyres must be unevenly worn and carry no more than half a millimetre of tread.

Fatalities on the Line

Nor are Formula One cars by any means the only vehicles that are fraught with obstacle and danger. The train can also be fatal, as I was reminded the other day at Winchester Station by an announcement regarding the delayed 17:22 to Portsmouth (I wasn't going to Portsmouth, obviously – nobody's ever been to Portsmouth – but the London trains were on the same electronic notice board).

It was late, said the notice board, 'due to an earlier fatality at Eastleigh'. I was furious. Not because of the delay, since it did not affect me, or anyone else I know, nor because of the late explanation, nor because of the selfishness of the suicide who chose the teeming Eastleigh rush hour for his (or, more probably, her) dramatic gesture, nor because of the unspecific nature of the excuse (it didn't say it was a suicide, so it might have been a fall from a carriage, a heart attack, a case of tuna-bap poisoning in the buffet car, or the first in a string of elaborate murders in a rolling *Murder on the Portsmouth Slow Train* whodunnit).

No, it was none of these – it was the word 'fatality'.

What is wrong with 'death'? Why such a clunky euphemism for an experience that will come to us all? It seems to have been plucked from the same periphrastic lexicon as 'African-American', 'learning difficulty' and 'same-sex lifestyle partner', as if death were something experienced only by the few, which the rest of us must circumlocute for fear of causing offence.

I was reminded of the way Nicholas Nickleby's headmaster at Dotheboys Hall gives him the news about his mother's death, which goes something like: 'Your mother is ill, boy ... She is very ill . . . In fact, she is extremely ill . . . She is dead.' Or, in the estuarised non-language of the British public announcement: 'She has experienced a fatality.'

What will they do when the dramatic impact of 'fatality' either ceases to resonate or itself becomes shocking (undergoes the sort of problem undergone by such words as 'coloured', 'gay' and 'spastic')? Will they move on to 'We are sorry your train is late, there has been a cessation of blood flow to the brain at Macclesfield'?

All new expressions eventually ossify into cliché and so, to save the rail fellows some effort, might I suggest the following alternative forms of expression: 'A customer at Newcastle Central has gone to sleep with Jesus'; 'A mortal coil has been shuffled off at West Jesmond'; 'After a long battle, the fight has been given up at Tiverton Parkway'; 'A bucket has been kicked at Bristol Temple Meads'; 'A Nuneaton commuter has tragically purchased the farm'; or – for war fans – 'Collateral damage has been sustained at Sandwell and Dudley'.

James Bond

I have always hated James Bond. For a long time my hatred of James Bond was the most interesting thing about me. Or, at least, it was the thing I most enjoyed wittering on about at dinner parties. And then they got Daniel Craig in, and *Casino Royale* was excellent, and it addressed most of the things that irritated me most about James Bond. And I thought that was that.

And then they made *Qunt and Her Solace* – as it was called before the censors moved in – and it was terrible, and we were right back where we started. And once again I hated James Bond.

I hate him because his iconic status resides in drinking, smoking and shagging. He is no more or less heroic than George Best. Calum Best, even.

And because he encourages the British cliché addiction – the need to hear the same thing over and over again. Catchphrases are only acceptable if they are funny. If every time he was asked his name he said 'chase me, chase me' or 'nice to see you, to see you . . . nice', then it might be OK.

Because every time a Bond film comes out we are told that it contains a new kind of 'feminist' Bond girl. And it never does.

Because Bond made it cool to be expelled from school – which is, in fact, the typical biographical detail of the useless upper-class layabout. The result is that Bond is a boor. His dismal one-liners might be a bit funnier if he had managed to stay at school.

Because, at least until Daniel Craig, Bond always had such a silly run. Connery's was like a swimwear model: all tippy-toe and exaggerated shoulder-bustle. Roger Moore had the defeated scamper of a wealthy old hairdresser fallen on hard times running after a bus because he didn't know you had to hail them from a bus stop, and Pierce Brosnan runs with the high-kneed trip and flapping elbows of the string-puppet milkmaid in the von Trapp family production of 'The Lonely Goatherd'.

Because Bond has made the very concept of tropical islands naff, fit only for Michael Winner, celebrity vote-out programmes and tabloid competition prizes. It was a short step from Ursula Andress in her bikini-and-dagger outfit to docusoaps about randy holiday reps.

Because Bond films ruined action movies by inventing the ten-minute unrelated action sequence before the plot starts to get the attention of illiterate morons.

Because in *You Only Live Twice* he says: 'You forget, Moneypenny, I took a first in oriental languages at Cambridge.' It is horribly uncool to reveal your degree score as an adult. And if he is so clever why is the only thing he says in Japanese in the whole film 'Donna Rigato', in a terrible European accent, as if it were the name of an Italian woman he fancied knocking off?

Because the release of a Bond film encourages the worst excesses of the 'Licence to Thrill' school of newspaper headline writing. How many 'Oh, Oh, Heaven' features about Bond girls do they think we can take?

Because he's a brilliant skier. Skiing is at worst a mindless Sloaney pastime for dingbats like Tara Palmer-Tomkinson and at best it's a keep-fit regime for dreary Austrians.

Because he seems to think that knowing about wine is somehow cool. But you only get to know that much by attending courses and reading books. It's no cooler than being a trainspotter. When Bond, in *Goldfinger*, says: 'My dear girl, there are some things that just aren't done. Such as drinking Dom Perignon '53 above a temperature of 38 degrees Fahrenheit,' he might as well be saying: 'My dear girl, in 1959 the A3-class Flying Scotsman was fitted with a Kylchap double exhaust arrangement and chimney to improve the steaming capability of the boiler with inferior coal.'

Because if people had been allowed to vote for James Bond in the '100 Greatest Britons' competition then he would almost certainly have won, which would have been almost as preposterous as Diana, Princess of Wales, winning, but not quite.

Because one in three male virgins has the Bond theme as his mobile phone ring tone.

Because whenever a new film comes out there is an interview with Roger Moore in which he is self-deprecating about his acting and makes lots of eyebrow jokes while you know that inside he is fuming because he thinks he's Laurence O-bleeding-livier.

Because the Bond PR machine always hints that the new film is this particular actor's last, and encourages speculation about possible successors (including bogus odds which you can't actually bet on). The list of 'possibles' always contains one pop singer (Robbie Williams), one actor who looks a bit like all the previous Bonds (Rufus Sewell), one black actor (Denzel Washington), one woman (Helen Mirren), one person who isn't an actor (David Beckham), one likely but boring candidate (Hugh Grant) and Mel Gibson.

Because Bond looks so stupid in a dinner jacket. The only time you wear a dinner jacket is for Oxford balls, Jewish weddings and cocktail parties in Denver.

Because James Bond reinforces the Hollywood myth that driving a car fast is big and clever, so teenage boys drive as fast as their car will go and end up killing themselves and their girlfriends and whole families walking on the pavement. And then when the council puts down speed bumps everyone complains that it's an infringement of civil liberties. If it weren't for Bond our roads would still be as flat as ironing boards.

Because James Bond is just Jeremy Clarkson with a better haircut and worse jokes.

Because in a week when the Gun Control Network launches a

campaigning poster featuring a man pointing a gun at a woman's head, most of Britain is blanketed with the same old posters of Bond and his bint pointing guns towards the camera. Shooting people to death just isn't entertaining.

Because you'll overhear some bore say that the films haven't been based on an Ian Fleming novel since *Octopussy*. And then someone will say 'that was a short story'. And then someone else will say 'and it was a completely different plot from the film, they just stole the name', and then you will shout, 'Oh for God's sake, the man couldn't write a shopping list', and then hate yourself for getting into conversation with those morons.

Because he plays table games in casinos. Only mugs do that. Roulette and baccarat involve no skill and all you're doing is feeding the percentage that is creamed off by the house. Table games are strictly for fat tourists from Nebraska. And so are Bond films.

Wheelie Luggage

It is the great irony of air travel that the posher the seats are, the more horrid the passengers. Heading for my economy seat through the club cabin, I always notice how the Business Class customers – about to enjoy a lovely pampered few hours – are the ones who simply won't move to let one by without a huge tut and grumble.

Business Class travellers have a sense of themselves as highly important individuals doing highly important things, and no sense of themselves as members of a wider community. No wonder they're the ones who complain. They have the fat, indolent sense of entitlement of aristocrats in pre-Revolutionary France. We should cut their effing heads off.

Perhaps the pampered ponces are sniffy about me because of my bag. You see, I always travel with a lovely, shiny, zip-top leather hold-all from Circa. And I carry it by the handles like a man. Not even a shoulder-strap. But Club men have wheelie carry-on luggage, to show that they are 'biznizmen' – as if their wan pallor, disdainful mien, dead eyes and fat bellies were not indication enough.

There is nothing manly or decent about wheelie luggage, and I hate to see it. With a huge trunk I suppose it's okay, if you're a woman. But not for men. Not with some weeny little overnight bag the size of a shoebox, full of men's cosmetics and ironed pants. I just can't bear to watch these hulking great, terribly important men with their minuscule bags on wheels scampering along behind them at the end of a long stick like some rectangular Chihuahua.

It's pathetic. Pick it up, man! How weak and lazy are you? Next thing you know they'll be making little wheelie wallets on long sticks so you can drag them behind you without all the effort of carrying it in your pocket. And wheelie phones. And wheelie pencils with one little wheel where the rubber used to be so you can drag it along the travelator, you lazy, pathetic bastard.

And what about wheelie money? Instead of carrying that huge, unwieldy tenner around with you everywhere, simply attach wheels to it and casually drag it down to the shops behind you. Along with several wheelie coins. And . . .

Messianic Politicians

Tony Blair won his general election in 1997 by persuading us that he was Jesus. Nobody remembers what the policies were; all we dimly recall is that he got angry when people said he didn't have any, insisted that he was not going to get into details, and promised to let us know what the policies were later. And we're still waiting. Some of us feel a little bit let down. We still think that he was Jesus, but in a bad way. In the wishy-washy, open-toed, passive-aggressive, turn-the-other-cheek, can't-touch-me-guv-I'm-with-the-Big-Guy way. The Messiah, but irritating.

David Cameron stands in a similar position today to that early, junior godhead Blair: he looks right, feels right, glows with a beatific something on which we cannot quite put our finger, but chooses to hold fire on policy and gets huffy when challenged to declare his ideological hand. If he were Jesus, this would be fine. But he is not.

Fortunately, though, it turns out he is Moses.

Or, rather, a 'direct descendant of Moses', as *The Times* reported recently, following the declaration of a Jewish scholar called Yaakov Wise that Cameron's great-great-grandfather Émile (surname 'Levita') was of the tribe of Levi. (I love the quasi-tautological concatenation of 'Jewish scholar'. You imagine the guy hunched round a candle in his prayer shawl and yarmulke, poring over the Cameron family tree.)

The tribe of Levi, as you probably know, are the descendants of Levi, the son of Jacob, who was the son of Isaac, who was the son of, oh ... wasn't he the son of Abraham? And wasn't

Abraham the first Jew – who changed his name from Abram to remind himself what he was not allowed to have in his sandwiches any more? So how does Moses fit in? I never get this right. He was in Exodus, wasn't he? He led them out of Egypt. Whereas Jacob is in Genesis, and had a son with an amazing coat whom he threw down a hole, from which he escaped up a ladder. Hang on, I'll have to check back to the article.

Okay, got it. This Wise fellow says, 'The leader of the Levites at the time of the Exodus was Moses . . . it is [thus] possible that Cameron is a direct descendant of Moses, or, at least, a cousin.'

Wow. That's pretty tenuous. A cousin. I'm a bit less excited than I was. Still, I think we can probably just about rebrand David Cameron as the long-awaited biblical leader of a nation, destined to lead his people into the Promised Land, don't you?

AND THERE went a man of the house of Levi, and took to wife a daughter of Levi. And the woman conceived, and bare a son: and when she saw him that he was a goodly child, fat and with that little twinkle old ladies simply adore, she took for him an ark of bulrushes, and put the child therein; and she laid it by the river's brink. And the daughter of Pharaoh came down and saw the ark; And when she had opened it, she saw the child: and she had compassion on him, and said, This is a Tory child. Poor little bleeder. And he became her son. And she called his name Moses: and she said, Let him mostly be known as Dave, for, let's face it, a kid called Moses will get hell at Eton.

AND THE angel of the LORD appeared unto Moses in a flame of fire out of the midst of a bush: and he looked, and, behold, the bush burned with fire, and the bush was not consumed. And Moses was relieved, for burning bushes were at that time the most significant source of greenhouse gases, and give off carbon dioxide like I don't know what.

And Moses saw that the LORD wanted him to compost where possible, and also recycle.

AND GOD came to Moses and saith; say unto the children of Israel, The LORD God of your fathers, hath sent me unto you: And I have said, I will bring you up out of the affliction of Egypt unto a land flowing with milk and honey. And Moses said, is it organic milk? I hope you have the name of the exact farm, because otherwise they will not touch it. Also there will need to be soya milk, unsweetened. For many of our women tolerate lactose not.

AND GOD said go. But Moses said, they will not believe me nor hearken unto my voice. And the LORD said unto him, What is that in thine hand? And he said, A rod. And the LORD said, It looks to me like a spliff. And Moses said, I have never confirmed or denied taking drugs during my time as a student. And He said, Cast it on the ground. And he cast it on the ground, and it became a serpent; and Moses fled from before it – lest it be an hallucination induced by the drugs he had neither confirmed nor denied any involvement withal. And the LORD said unto Moses, Put forth thine hand, and take it by the tail. And he put forth his hand, and caught it, and it became a rod in his hand: That they may believe that the LORD God of their fathers hath appeared unto thee. And Moses said, but what happened to my spliff?

AND MOSES went unto Pharaoh and said, Let my People go! And Pharaoh said, Thou willst have to be more specific. And Moses said, Let my People go to the Cotswolds for the weekend. And Pharaoh said, Is that all? You should have said. Fine, no problem. As long as they're back for work on Monday – those pyramids are not going to build themselves. And Moses, said: Let my People go until the Tuesday so they can do a spot of hunting and have a top supper in the village pub and not get stuck in traffic on the M4. And Pharaoh said, Don't push it, Sunshine.

AND PRETTY soon the people had all fallen in behind Moses, except one or two Egyptians who did not want to put a windmill on their houses, for they would spoil the pointy pyramidal look of the place. And these deniers of global warming chased the Tories with their 4x4s but the LORD caused the sea to go back and made the sea dry land, and the waters were divided. And the Egyptians pursued, and went in after them to the midst of the sea, and were drowned. Even all Pharaoh's Porsche Cayennes and BMW X5s and their drivers. And Moses said unto the LORD, I hope you know what you are doing, messing with the finely balanced ecosystem of our precious ocean resource. If any blue-fin tuna have been harmed, I'll have hell to answer for.

AND THE children of Israel came into the wilderness of Sinai. And the LORD came down upon Mount Sinai, and the LORD called Moses up to the top of the mount; and Moses went up to hear His commandments. And afterwards Moses went down unto the people, with his tablets, and spake unto them, saying: Thou shalt . . .

AND THEN he paused, saying: On second thoughts, let's leave these till after the election.

Bullfighting

If Greta Scacci wants to pose naked with a cod to promote sustainable fishing, then that's absolutely fine with me. I am a committed and vociferous campaigner for responsible ocean management, and I love looking at pictures of naked ladies. For me, it's a win–win situation. 'Get your kecks off, Gret,' I say, 'and tell it like it is.' But when Ricky Gervais throws his oar in with the anti-bullfighting lobby, declaring that 'Bullfighting needs to stop, it's so cruel', then the waters, for me, are not so clear.

If, for example, he is going to take off his clothes and bare his capacious arse for the camera wearing nothing but a pair of party horns to draw attention to his opinions, then I want no part of it. I do not like looking at naked old men and, as it happens, I enjoy bullfighting.

I would love to be able to write that sentence – 'I enjoy bullfighting' – without qualification or apology, and then just tear into Ricky's sentimental, bone-headed outburst, brimming as it was with all the paternalistic condescension of Britain's darkest imperial days, but I am not an idiot. I know that most of you are pretty squeamish about bullfighting yourselves. You are, after all, the people who give more money to donkey sanctuaries than you do to African children rendered parentless by AIDS.

So I must provide my apologia in advance, and explain why my support of the Spanish bullfight is entirely compatible with my great respect for (rather than soupy 'love of') animals, and with my ongoing support for better animal husbandry in the food industry. And why it doesn't make me cruel.

'What is the pleasure in seeing an animal speared to death?'

Gervais asked, entirely rhetorically, not expecting an answer. But, Ricky, since you ask, I'll tell you that there is no pleasure in 'seeing an animal speared to death', per se. There is sadness. And the bullfight invites you to confront the sadness. Death is awful. You've no doubt heard.

The Spanish (not all the Spanish, but most) think it is better to confront it, in this way and in others (flamenco claims to confront the pain of death also, but I have never grasped how), than to suppress it, to flab around in an office all day making smart remarks and then shuffle off to a comedy theatre to hear some paunchy twat from Reading tell you what he thinks is funny about MPs' expenses claims.

I enjoy bullfighting, as millions of Spaniards do, in spite of the pain caused to the animal, not because of it. That is a crucial, and by no means a specious distinction. If I ever kill a man (and I really hope that I don't), it will be because I have a reason to do so, not because I enjoy it. And I will be sentenced accordingly.

Thus, at the bullring, in return for the sadness of witnessing an animal killed, I am rewarded with a thrill far more visceral than you'll experience at any sporting event or pop concert. There is the throb of ancient history and tradition, the celebrated beauty of blood and sand, red and gold, and the pure lines of movement that enthralled Picasso – the great atavistic ballet. I get the fear of human death (unlikely post-penicillin, but still possible), and the thrill of its avoidance, and then the death of the bull, which is as inevitable as mine and yours. And throughout, that proximity to the bloody and barbaric birth of our visual culture, to the hell of the Roman Coliseum, that I would otherwise never know.

Have you ever seen a terrified bull killed by a tattooed tractor boy with a fag in his mouth in a stinking East Anglian abattoir? I have. Plenty. And you don't get any of those things. Just the sadness. Just the sick feeling. And a mountain of burger meat lying in its own post-mortal crap.

Gervais eats meat, for Heaven's sake. I can accept an onslaught on bullfighting from a vegan. I have nothing to counter the accusation of cruelty from a person who forgoes all the pleasures of the plate and condemns himself to a life of bean-eating, totally abasing himself before the entire animal kingdom because of his overwhelming sympathy for it. Such a man (or, more likely, woman) has my respect. It is they who will save the world, in between frantic dashes to the toilet, noisily to pebble dash the pot with last night's spicy aubergine and lentil ragout.

But meat-eaters like Gervais have not a leg to stand on. We have become so separated by urbanisation from the process of our food production that we have discounted multiple animal carnage for meat as a moral thing at all. We (well, you) are moved to tears by the public slaughter of a dumb beast with a bit of ceremony and a *paso doble* a thousand miles away, but dare not confront the thousands of hidden deaths much closer to home which it takes to feed your belly.

A bull bred to fight lives wild on the range, in the herd, untouched by man, eating what it wants, getting laid occasionally, until, when it is five or six years old, it is rounded up and taken to town to fight and die. The Spanish will say, 'to fulfil its destiny', but let's not get silly.

A bull bred for your Sunday lunch, on the other hand, or for your grabbed midnight burger on a pissed-up Thursday night, lives mostly indoors. Like Ricky Gervais. It lives on silage. And then, when it is no more than three years old, it is taken out and shot. Like a deserter. Do you really feel better about that?

You who are so quick to anthropomorphise the bull and weepily to share its pain, try reversing the process. Imagine not that the bull is a man, but that you are the bull. Imagine that you are given the choice between living to, say, 35 years of age, mostly in a shed, in massive single sex groups, feeding on silage (prison is a fair comparison), and then queuing with your mates to die at the hand of a shaven-headed thug with a bolt gun . . .

Or then again, imagine living free in thousands of acres of

land, eating whatever you want, shagging who you like, and then, when you are perhaps 70, being asked to fight to the death against a Spaniard in pink tights.

Sure, the morning of your 70th birthday, when you wake up and it's time to meet your maker, you're going to think, 'oh, crap'. But would you honestly give back those 35 years of real living to have some beefy half-trained yokel blow your brains out with a pistol?

Ricky Gervais made his millions by celebrating the Englishman at his most vain, pompous, small-minded, insular and bigoted. His humour is built on the sneer. On inspired displays of passive-aggressive wit at the unfamiliar, in defence of blubby middle England, a grey archipelago of mini-roundabouts and miserable desk-jockeys living on Greggs pies and surfing a little surreptitious porn at teatime.

Of course he doesn't like bullfighting! Too much colour, too much history, too much life, too much death, too much blood and sand, too much foreignness, too much difference. I dare say he doesn't like paella either, or frogs' legs, bratwurst, haiku, poncey foreign novels, French poetry or snooty classical music composed by krauts, funny-looking Portuguese people, wanky Italian opera, sushi . . .

I know that every celeb needs an animal to hug in public, but I'll vote with naked Greta and her nice bit of cod over fat Rick and his misplaced suburban sentimentality anytime.

Christmas Book Round-Ups

One Sunday morning last year, about a month before Christmas, I was curled up on the sofa reading Sarah Waters's *The Little Stranger*, and enjoying it very much indeed, thank you very much, when I paused briefly to flick through the papers and found myself mired in one of those wretched 'Books of the Year' features. Seeing *The Little Stranger* mentioned, I looked idly down to see what was said about it and read, 'A poltergeist wreaks havoc in this wonderfully atmospheric horror tale . . .'

Eh? A poltergeist? Not in *The Little Stranger* I was reading. At least, not in the first 150 pages. Ah. Those funny marks on the wall and the ceiling. The unlikely savaging of the small child by the docile dog. The housemaid's irrational fear of the back stairs. That was because of . . . a poltergeist? I had no idea it was even a ghost story. I had no idea it was anything but a conventional novel about normal things. So that was my reading experience spoiled. £16.99 down the Swanee because my Sunday paper couldn't be bothered to commission actual journalism so 'close' to Christmas.

Not that they'd care. Christmas book round-ups are not designed to serve readers. They are designed to get pages full nice and early so staff can put on paper hats and have a slap-up Turkey Twizzler lunch. And to allow pompous celebrities to show off about the one book they read all year, and call it 'towering', or, 'by turns lyrical and profound'.

Who reads books now anyway? Nobody. One just gives them as presents and hopes not to get any in return. That's why book-of-the-year round-ups don't come at the end of the year any more. Readers have to have time to buy the book online and send it as a present to someone in time for them to rewrap it and give it to the person who will eventually take it down to Oxfam, dust their hands off with a smile and reckon that that's their bit done for starving children for another year.

When I did my first Christmas books ring-round for *The Times* in 1993, they published it on Christmas Eve, because back then the rule was that you couldn't fill what was supposed to be a newspaper with a lot of witless padding until it was actually Christmas. The one that spoiled my recent Sunday was published on 29 November. And it was by no means the first. They've been rounding up books of the year since September. And the poor old work-experience kids that have to do it probably started in the summer, before they had to go back to school. And then, of course, the celebs needed the time to read the books (lips moving, fingers sliding along the lines). These 'Books of the Year' are nothing more than 'The Books of the First Three Months of the Year Up Until the End of March'. The whole thing is a sham.

But not as much of a sham as the old 'hints for spicing up that Christmas dinner' routine. Ye Gods, the old hams they wheel out for that (hello again, Delia), telling us to ram a handful of medlar compote up the poor bird's arse and pretend it's 1485. Or to think of serving, yawn, goose instead. Or a rib of horse. Or what about a nice sea bass in ginger and chilli to make a change from boring old turkey?

Make a change? It's only once a bloody year! How can one possibly need a break from the monotony of eating something once every 12 months? At the age of 40, there is no other dish I can think of that I have eaten only 36 times. Turkey, potatoes, sprouts, Christmas pudding. Fine. The reason it has not evolved is because there have been only about 130 Christmases since it was invented. In 'eating time', the roast turkey dinner is less than five months old. It is simply not in need of being jazzed up by a supplement full of celebrity pan-bashers.

And why do men wear their scarves in such a dumb way nowadays? I bought myself a scarf for the first time in years the other day and flung it round my neck, Dr Who-style, as one should, only to suddenly become aware that every other man in London was wearing theirs like a sort of cravat, doubled over and then both ends reversed through the loop to make a neat little lapel-filling bundle. Not mimsy little Eyeties, mind. Englishmen!

What sort of bizarre collective unconscious thing saw to that? One minute we're wrapping a long woollen thing round our neck to keep it warm, next thing you know everyone's mincing around with a girly bloody great knot in their scarf and the end tucked into their coats, like Beau bleeding Brummell in a frock coat and stock. Makes me sick.

And what the hell is Merry Wobs? Don't tell me, I know. It's like 'dual off' and 'shiv' and 'total aunt', isn't it? It's like 'book' for 'cool' and 'zonino' for 'woohoo'. It's what you get when you type 'xmas' into a predictive phone, isn't it? It must be. I wouldn't know, because I wouldn't type 'xmas' in the first place because I'm not a moron who thinks he's too busy to write 'Christmas'.

Bag, gunbug.

Snow

A blanket of snow covers my back garden. But if you change 'blanket' to 'vomit', it doesn't sound quite so nice, does it? The mysterious power of words. And it's far closer to the truth. You can't pull this blanket off, can you? You can't fold it up and put it away? You can't eat a picnic on it. It was just sprayed out in a great gush last night after a party and will lie around looking all messy until someone goes out there and cleans it up. And it's not going to be me, because I didn't do it.

My north-facing, North London garden is the coldest place on earth at the best of times. Now it looks like the North Pole (brown and gritty with a tiny bit of melting snow). It looks like there ought to be polar bears out there. They could make friends with the fox. It would be like a Glacier Mints advert. Except with the fox all mangy and grey, with one lame leg and a KFC box in its mouth.

My garden doesn't get much above five degrees even in high summer, what with the constant shadow and the icy winds swooshing down through Highgate from the Urals. Every exposed surface – trees, benches, windows, the gardener's face – is lichened to the colour of a Martian's arse. In August, when everyone else has a hosepipe ban, I'm cracking the ice on the water butt with an axe, scraping frost off the roses, donating jumpers to homeless charities and making porridge.

So this Dickensian throwback to the days when snow fell at Christmas, the Thames froze and birds fell stiff from the trees and smashed on the road like wine glasses has not pleased me. I spent most of the summer having a lovely old-fashioned larder built against the north-east wall of the kitchen, and now I'm having to bring all the food out of it and put it in the fridge so that it doesn't freeze, like an Eskimo. (Honestly, that's what Eskimos use fridges for: to stop their food freezing. It was one of my favourite facts from a book called *Crazy But True* when I was about eight years old. I was always disturbing my dad with amazing things from it, like how the average man grows thirty feet of whiskers in a lifetime, and how it once rained mashed potato in Kent. He said they should have called it *Crazy But Wrong*.)

When the first, cautious gusts of snow began to swirl on Wednesday, my girlfriend burst into the room and cried, 'Snow!' Then Caitlin Moran twittered, 'Snow! I'm quitting my job, putting brandy in my coffee and building a sledge!' Suddenly, my inbox was engulfed in a blizzard of round-robin 'OMG!'s from bored female journalists who spend all winter staring out the window, scanning the skies for evidence of anomalous precipitation, like air-raid wardens reassigned by some dark conglomerate of the Met Office, Raymond Briggs and Aled Jones, all shrieking about sleigh bells and Bing Crosby and Charles Dickens and God knows what else.

The street filled instantaneously with children, bursting out of every door, in little scarves and earmuffs, arms outstretched, swirling in glee like Julie Andrews in the high Alps, straight out into the traffic . . . HONK!!! Screeeeeeeeech!!! Lucky not to be wiped off the surface of England by drivers all gawping up at the sky like they'd never seen a frozen water droplet before. I swear, most road accidents in snowy weather are caused not by skids, but by drivers staring upwards instead of looking where they're going. I'll wager people don't get hit by cars much in snowy weather in Norway. No, because after ten thousand years they have finally got the hang of just CARRYING ON AS NORMAL!

And yet it's not all a bed of snowy roses in Norway, I can tell you. And all these snow-lovers with their woolly hats and their stupid mittens and their accursed fluffy red earmuffs should think twice before wishing that it snowed as much here as it does there because I can tell you what happens when it does. I was there a couple of years ago in the early spring, right at the start of the thaw. And you know what it was? It was defrosted dog-turd hell.

Now, it's bad enough in England when a fine blanket of snow settles on the world, and you step out into the street and immediately hit your first concealed urban dog sausage of the season – squelch, skid, puke – or when you take a toboggan up onto the Heath and positively plummet down hillsides of hound crap and then come home to spend the evening listening to Nat King Cole and drinking mulled wine as you scrape eight kilos of putrefied Winalot from the runners. But in Norway, ye gods!

What happens in Oslo is that all winter long the lazy sodding dog-owners, who can't be bothered to bend down and clean up on a cold morning (they're the same as the ones here except taller, with blonde hair and patterned jumpers), just let the dogs squeeze out their worst, knowing that in minutes the evidence will have been covered by fresh snow. All winter this goes on. Poo after poo after poo, layering up under leaves of snow like some hellish lasagne. For months!

And then the thaw comes. All at once, the snow melts, and there, at your feet, is eight months of dog poo, perfectly preserved and ready to crack out its baby fresh whiff at the first sight of sunshine. Every last inch, covered. As if one giant dog the size of Texas had decided to squat over Oslo and unload its breakfast.

That's what happens when it snows a lot. That is the untold story behind the lovely wintry scenes on a billion Christmas cards. That's what good King Wenceslas looked out upon, immediately beneath the old 'deep and crisp and even'. That's what is beneath Bing's feet as he sings, and what gets trodden into his front room in the spring. That's what lies beneath the ground as hard as iron, my friends. 'In the bleak midwinter, frosty wind made moan, Earth stood hard as iron, concealing all the pone' ('pone' – Cockney rhyming slang: 'pony and trap').

And anyway, snow kills old people. And, worse, it ruins your shoes. And you can't get anywhere. And they give children the day off school so they can loiter about at the end of your garden, struggling to light their crack pipes in big mittens. And then it piles up in the gutters looking all grey and messy. And there is always the half-decayed, grey and gritty body of a dead snowman, slumped in the local playground, from which the snow has long since receded, with its hat fallen off and its pipe askew, looking like the remains of a lynched paedophile.

And then, weeks after the London thaw, you see the odd Volvo sitting in traffic in town with an inch of snow on the roof and you think, 'Where the hell have you come in from, Reykjavik?'

And then you go home to your house in the coldest street in North London, and step out into your north-facing garden, and you're up to your knees in snow. And it stays there till June.

(My girlfriend just came in again, by the way, all excited this time because there were pretty icicles hanging from the roof. I agreed that was very exciting. And then I went out on to the roof to crack the ice in the gutters so the bedroom doesn't flood.)

Sex

It is offensive, reductive and patently unprovable to suggest, as common opinion has it, that men think about sex, on average, every six seconds.

It may be true of your acne-riddled 13-year-old knob-frotter, still bug-eyed and panting from his first bean-flick, who hasn't got anything else to think about anyway and decorates his bedroom with posters of topless models, all smooth and golden-skinned with full, meaty breasts and trim little pussies with just a tangle of auburn hair in which to twine their long-nailed fingers. But the suggestion that a grown man like me (who gets plenty of it regularly, thank you very much) can't live through a tenth of a minute of his working day without thinking about the smooth buttocks of underage Thai girls mud-wrestling in Bailey's, is an insulting cliché perpetuated by women, explicitly to undermine the professional and social credibility of men.

I'm a columnist on the world's oldest national newspaper, for Christ's sake. A respected man. Giles Coren of *The Times*. How could I possibly maintain my position if I was unable to sustain periods of deep philosophical reflection for longer than five seconds without thinking about putting my cock in something?

I have to keep abreast (*mmmmm*, 'breasts') of the news. You think I'd ever get any work done if every time I went down (*mmmm*, 'went down') to check the hourly bulletin I was overcome by fantasies of Emily Maitlis in rubber boots and a pleated hockey skirt playing bell-end ping-pong with Huw Edwards? You think if my head was full of her plump, glistening lips, porn-bronze skin and long eyelashes gazing up at his big

Welsh ball bag, playfully flicking one bollock and then the other with her darting, slippery tongue, that I'd be able to maintain a firm grasp (*mmmm,* 'firm grasp') on the state of the nation? Ye gods, I'd never finish an article. Somebody else's column would end up plugging my slot (*mmmmm,* 'pluggi . . .', no, wait, that's not good).

Every six seconds, I ask you. It just isn't feasible. What about when I'm playing football in Regent's Park? That's just 90 minutes of pure Corinthian toil, unsullied by even a milli-moment of putrid lechery. Do you think that in the frequent lulls to catch my breath after darting diagonal runs worthy of a man half my age (*mmmm,* 'half my age') if I happen to catch sight of a young mum wheeling her baby towards the zoo (*mmmm,* 'the zoo'), I pause even momentarily to stare at her rolling, fecund hips and fantasise about rescuing her child from a marauding Doberman so that she takes me back to her place to show me how grateful she is?

You think it even occurs to me to imagine easing her jeans down over the mottled and creamy maternal flesh and making sweet love to her while the rescued toddler plays with its Lego in the room next door? What kind of monster do you think I am?

And what about when I'm driving? I am hardly likely to be thinking about sex then. I am the most disciplined and single-minded driver you have ever known. Great driving is all about driving defensively: slow to first gear at every intersection and look both ways before proceeding smoothly to . . . HOT DANG! Would you get a load of the tumblers on that! Set them free, darling, that's cruelty to puppies that is! You could pick locks with nipples like that. Shouldn't be allowed.

I am not saying that men don't think about sex occasionally. Sex is everywhere: adverts, pop videos, shop windows, gardening programmes, chessboards (the hooters on that queen), pork pies (*mmmmm,* 'pork'), phones, spoons, rolls of Sellotape, mountains, eggs, pencils, I mean, Christ, it's not me that's sex-mad, it's the culture. You'd have to be Oliver Cromwell not to get a hard-on just listening to the *Today* programme on Radio 4 (*mmmm*, 'aggressive banter in bed').

I am happily bound in a relationship and outside that pretty much a monk in the rumpy department. I would never go into a lap-dancing club, for example, but if I'm driving up London's Tottenham Court Road past Spearmint Rhino and suddenly there is a great big poster of a woman in a pink negligee prowling horizontally across a shag-pile carpet with her powerful, bronzed thighs, all sweet-scented and lickable in scary shoes, then is that really me thinking about sex?

Am I thus complicit in the shameful exploitation of the chain? Am I, by proxy, a seedy little turd who has to get his rocks off ogling smacked-out Croatian refugees for banknotes? If, as a result of seeing their demeaning and sexist advertisement, I am forced to pull over into the first available legitimate parking space and knock one out into a clean handkerchief, am I to be considered in cahoots?

Six seconds, really? The truth is that most days I don't give sex so much as a second thought for hours at a time. Blow job. Especially if I'm working. Indeed I think I have proved that very point by writing this article without giving shyly teased clitorises or sexily fingered perinea even the briefest mention. So if you'll forgive a brief closing aperçu on the semantic paradoxicality of the temporo-sexual conundrum, qua cliché, as it is refracted through phallogocentric feminist discourse in the writings of . . .

Bugger. One of those little dancing girl pop-ups has appeared on my screen, totally uninvited, and looks all plump and bulbous in her cartoon bikini – you'd never guess she was just a drawing (*mmmmm*, 'Jessica Rabbit'). But that's not fair, that's not me thinking about sex, that's some pervy Internet zip-file cache-thing bloggo person thinking about it. I will not, at the final hurdle, be distracted from . . . *mmmm*, she's rather nice actually. She's never going to take off those . . . she is as well. I wonder what happens if you click on . . . wow. Shit, sorry. I'm going to have to go and um you know, er . . . how many seconds is that?

People Who Think They Have a Book in Them

The poet Shelley famously declared that 'Poets are the unacknowledged legislators of the world'. That's the *poet* Shelley, you notice. As opposed to the fishmonger Shelley, who no doubt thought that fishmongers were the unacknowledged legislators of the world, or the proctologist Shelley who no doubt made the same high claim for proctologists. And might well have been right.

But if poets are not quite all that Shelley claimed (and with a first name like 'Percy' and a middle name like 'Bysshe' he was bound to have self-worth issues), I think it is fair to say that poets are certainly the ultimate custodians of our expressive originality. It is the job of poets and of creative writers generally (since nobody gives an arse for poets any more; I mean, come on, name a living poet – apart from Pam Ayres) constantly to push the possibilities of language, to find new ways of saying things, to kill off old forms, hackneyed metaphor, desiccated imagery, to prosecute the war on cliché.

So isn't it odd that there are more clichés attached to the business of writing than to almost anything else? Apart from death and fucking, of course, about which nobody has said anything new for a thousand years.

Think of when you're looking at the back of a book, wondering whether to buy it or not: those little recommendations from Nick Hornby and Salman Rushdie and Kathy Lette. They're always the same: 'A rattling good read', 'I couldn't put it down', 'it kept me awake until four in the morning', 'actually made me laugh out loud on the Tube . . .'

What does it matter that a piece of creative writing kept Kathy Lette awake until four in the morning? A dodgy car alarm can do that. Who cares what makes Salman Rushdie laugh out loud on the Tube? A good joke about tits would be enough, I'm sure.

And then there are the more general critical clichés: 'all first novels are autobiographical', 'he's got classic second novel syndrome', 'writing is a form of catharsis'. It's just meaningless arty turd.

And then, of course, there are the brutish, dismissive clichés. There is a sort of person who, when you tell them, 'I'm writing a novel', replies: 'Neither am I.' This kind of person is a *Private Eye* reader who read the gag in a cartoon twenty years ago and still thinks it's funny because he is crippled by the knowledge that he will never do anything worthwhile with his own puny little life and has to believe that nobody else will either, just to be able to get up in the morning.

People used to say that last one to me all the time. But I *was* writing a novel, and I finished it, and it was published. So they can all fuck off. It was about a miserable young man called Winkler with a filthy ugly girlfriend and a shit job (but a very high opinion of himself), who has a tendency to wank in front of blind women and finally pushes a fat bird under a train to see if it will make him happier, and it does. And if anyone tells me: 'Coren's first novel is, of course, autobiographical', they can have a poke in the eye.

Which brings me to the notion that 'Everyone has a book in them'. Fine. That is probably the best place for it. Keep it there. Do not attempt to write it down. The world has too many books already, just as it has too many people.

People are boring, and they do not have stories inside them or anything else apart from blood, water and poo. At best, everyone has inside them a boring anecdote to deliver in the pub when everyone else is too pissed to remember it in the morning. And even then, I'm sceptical.

The belief that everyone has a book inside them is what led Iain Duncan-Smith, for example, to write one. And Ann Widdecombe, and Douglas Hurd, and William Hague. And all that ever proved, all the way back to Winston Churchill and Benjamin Disraeli, is that everybody has a dreary old Tory MP inside them. Another former Tory MP, Edwina Currie, has written dozens of books. And all she ever had inside her was John Major.

And it's not just that lot who were mistaken in the belief that they had a novel in them. Jeffrey Archer never had one, did he? It was other people who had those novels in them and Jeffers just did the typing. In fact, I've heard it said he didn't even do that.

And have you ever tried to read a novel by Henry James? I don't know what he had inside him, but it sure as hell wasn't books. And who told that dreary fat old greasebag Umberto Eco he had a novel in him? A film, yes, *The Name of the Rose*. But only because of that naked peasant girl's stupendous jubblies.

And who told Samuel Beckett 'ooh, that sounds like fun, you should write a play'? And who thought Samuel Richardson had a book in him? Or Thackeray? Or Anthony Powell? Or George Eliot? Or Alexander Solzhebloomingnitsyn?

I'm not saying that nobody has a book inside them. Nick Hornby had a book in him. But why has he written eight? He was an Arsenal fan with a very good book about Arsenal in him. That was no reason to let the others out.

A writer isn't a person with some boring arse life story who just puts it down on paper because he thinks people ought to hear about it. He is a person who tells stories other people want to read, wherever they come from. He makes them up from things he sees – such as blind girls, fat birds, masturbation and trains.

I have written a book. I plan to write more. But I have never had a book in me. Not even this one.

Women Who Claim to Find Funny Men Attractive

If I hear another woman as long as I live say that what she finds most sexy in a man is the ability to make her laugh, I swear, I shall throttle her to death with my whoopee cushion. Because it just isn't true. It is yet another dismal cliché of the feminist backlash derived from the infuriating truism that men are shallow and clumsy whereas women are deep and esoteric. But it's bollocks. If women really went for funny men then Woody Allen wouldn't have had to marry his own daughter.

What women want is not a man who makes them laugh, but a man who makes them rich. Or would you like me to believe that Slavia Ecclestone just can't get enough of Bernie's knock-knock jokes and that Jane Fonda fell for Ted Turner when she heard him sing 'God Bless America' on helium? It is diamonds that are a girl's best friend. Not limericks. Not itching powder. Not reruns of *Seinfeld*. Diamonds.

And if not money, then height. Women like tall. You can tell the crappest joke in the world but if you tell it from six feet seven off the floor you can take your pick from the ladies listening. There is nothing clever or sophisticated about it. If a man is tall then he may have a larger than average cock, and if not he will at least be able to reach your hat down from the shelf above the coats.

What women want is a tall, rich, good-looking, ideally famous, man with a big cock who is comfortable talking about his feelings. Funny they can get from one of their lame-arse Doris-oriented television programmes like *Sex in the City* or *30 Rock*. You think Magic Johnson lost count of the number of birds he had shagged because he was the Dick Emery of the NBA? You think Tiger Woods wooed all those Las Vegas hostesses with hilarious quotations from P.G. Wodehouse?

Women think they are so sophisticated and worldly with their 'funny men are the sexiest' crap. But it's all a hoax to make us believe they are more complicated than we are. A man falls for a woman because her bum looks nice in a pair of tangerine knickers, but a woman falls for a man because he knows seven or eight Python sketches by heart? I don't think so. If women find funny men so attractive, then why did Hill's Angels always run away, and why did Benny die cold and alone?

These women who are so hung up on funny men – are these the ones who, when we were fifteen and tried to impress them with funny faces and fart noises, rolled their eyes and whined: 'Oh grow up!', and then trotted off to screw some 25-year-old yuppie with a Porsche?

Are they the ones who, when we were nine, failed to see the funny side of stink bombs and went running to their Barbie cupboards to drag out poor, dumb plastic Ken and stroke him, weeping, dreaming of the day when they could marry a mute, lantern-jawed fuckwit of their own who would never expect them to laugh at a funny smell?

When did you ever hear a woman laugh? Come on, when? Unless it's at a bad shirt you were going to wear to a wedding or a failed attempt to cook them dinner? Women don't have a sense of humour. That's why they don't tell jokes. They have an interest in shoes instead. It's just the way they're wired. You can be telling the best fucking joke in the world (the one where the little girl being dragged into the woods at night by a dirty old man says, 'I'm scared' and he replies: 'You're scared? I've got to walk back on my own . . .'), but if she catches sight of a pair of décolleté jazz pumps by Louboutin at 25 per cent off in a shop window, it's as if you weren't even fucking born.

How can women judge a man by his sense of humour when

women don't even get jokes? You tell a woman a joke and she'll always say, 'Is that true or did you make it up?' or 'What was the relevance of his being Welsh?'

Worse still, women have whole fields of things marked out in their mind about which it is not acceptable to make jokes. These include: war, famine, death, paedophilia, genocide, animal cruelty, female body parts, marital fidelity, their friends, their family, the ugliness of George Eliot, women's sports, homelessness, old age, disability, mental illness, foreign people's accents, homosexuality . . . I mean, what the fuck is left to be funny about? Diets? Fake tanning products? Personal shoppers?

Worst of all, women are unable to laugh at themselves. This is because they are so busy trying to be taken seriously in all the areas of life about which men no longer give a fuck: the workplace, politics, the army, the City, the MCC . . . the things which used to matter to men until we thought, fuck it, let's leave it to the ladies. Women are to the 21st century what those dour, humourless, hard-working stuffy old bastard men were to the 19th. And they don't want a funny husband any more than those old gits wanted a funny wife.

Listen, I am a funny man. Not fall on the floor, clutch your sides, stamp and vomit and weep funny, like Eddie Izzard or Les Dawson or that bloke with the hairy hands who presents the football on Sky, but funny enough. I know some quite good jokes and can do them with voices. I am sharper than your average geezer with the one-liners, the put-downs, the low-brow mutterings that can often raise a laugh at the opera, the Francophobic gag shouted into a lull at the footie. And yet I can count the women who have fallen for me in my life on the fingers of one hand. And still have two left to pick my arse.

So what do I do now? Get rich? Get tall? Get sensitive? Or adopt a daughter?

Music

No cliché begins life as a cliché. It starts off, generally speaking, as a witty aperçu which causes people to nod and say, 'Oh you're so right' or, 'I wish I'd thought of that', and to walk home determined to remember it and repeat it later when conversation is flagging at a party and a pretty girl is standing there, looking as if she might be waiting for someone to say something crisp, witty and original. It is only after endless repetition that it becomes a cliché, and thus worthless, without meaning, a semantic black hole.

The first man that ever said 'football is a game of two halves' probably stopped that cocktail party in its tracks. On hearing it, Noel Coward no doubt turned to Dorothy Parker and said: 'It is, you know'. There may even have been a patter of quiet applause. And I believe it was Oscar Wilde who, after Bury's shock 4–0 defeat of Southampton in the FA Cup Final of 1900, remarked that 'there are no easy games at this level.'

'It's six of one, half a dozen of the other, mate,' said Talleyrand, when Napoleon asked if he thought winter was a good time to march on Moscow, to which Napoleon, staggered by the clarity of Talleyrand's appraisal, replied: 'Fuck it, then – let's do it!'

But as time passes, repetition by morons (keen to enliven their dreary mortal speech as much as to avoid saying anything of their own which might get them in trouble) turns these phrases to dust. And so it is with the assertion that 'all art constantly aspires towards the condition of music'.

I do not blame Walter Pater, the great Victorian aesthete, for first asserting it. He spent his life trying to pin down the intrinsic nature of art – 'to burn always with this hard, gem-like flame' – to explain why art alone can approach the fundamental truths of the human experience. He failed, of course, which is why modern art is about cutting fish in half and piling elephant poo on gallery floors.

Pater and his fellow aesthetes were looking for sublimity, a form of artistic truth that could be said to affect the senses without mediation by the corruptive influences of the intellect. Literature required too much thought to mediate pure feeling, while painting and sculpture – static as they were – were bereft of the power to move.

But to be moved by music you need only to hear, not to process. You need no education to appreciate tunes. It is the most democratic of arts. The dumbest sister-shagging hillbilly in Oklahoma, the scariest redneck, will weep at 'Stand By Your Man' or the theme from *The Dukes of Hazzard*. Just as any old twonk can be moved by Albinoni's Adagio in G minor. Can't get through *Madame Bovary*? Try nine minutes of Mozart.

Music's unarguable cultural primacy in the world today was achieved because in the twentieth century the masses finally won over the intellectuals, the dumb over the sensitive, the witless over the witty, and the mass-produced over the finely wrought. Far from art aspiring to the condition of music, music is the art form for people who are too thick to appreciate any of the others.

I've never been to a 'gig' in my life. Nor to the opera or the Festival Hall. People offer me tickets and I politely decline, on the grounds that music is shit. 'But, Giles,' they say, 'all art constantly aspires towards the condition of music'.

Oh really? So what Tolstoy really wanted to achieve artistically was the condition of some bloke in a pimped Vauxhall with a doo rag on his head bobbing like a nodding dog to some drivelling bass line while he leers at passing bitches, but unfortunately he fell short and only managed *Anna Karenina*?

I hate music. I hate people in church choirs standing there all pious, looking up at the ceiling, warbling away with their mouths formed into great big Os like a camel blowing smoke rings. They get like that from sucking the choirmaster's cock from an early age, you know.

I hate musicians, those violinists looking all serious as they scratch their strings, head wobbling and scowling like gorillas. The pianists swaying about on their stools, the stupid clarinettists with their miserable turned-down faces.

Music is for wide-arsed desk-jockeys in four-year-old Rovers to keep themselves awake on the drive home – flooring the gas pedal as they ease off the slip road onto the M25 in sympathy with the sudden striking up of the chorus to 'Bat Out of Hell'. You really think that's what Milton aspired to?

Did Leonardo dream of a world enslaved by the iPod, which, along with its predecessor the Walkman, has – by locking each citizen in his own aural world – been the prime mover in the collapse of social fluidity based on interpersonal communication. Look at the behavioural problems caused by undiagnosed deafness in children, and you have a picture of where the iPod is taking mankind. Music is for hopeless, marginalised morons. Why else is your drug-dealer's other job DJ-ing? He's not a sonneteer, is he? Or a limner?

And music leads to dancing. And dancing is the devil's work. Never do I feel more alone than when I see my friends blended into the roiling throng, tossing their hair around their heads, staring at their feet and at the sky, legs and arms moving without reason or directional intent. There is no will to communicate in this – which is the defining privilege of the human; no possibility of distilling meaning from the stinking animal soup that bubbles there. Only the wild orgy of movement before death.

All art does not aspire to this. Give me a good book every time. Or even a bad one.

Mates

I shouldn't do this. I shouldn't give so much away. I could just tell you I had loads of great mates, not a bad word to say, solid geezers, salt of the earth, never had any trouble on that score, and be done. I could tell you: 'Birds, I can take or leave, but a real mate is there for life.' That's what I ought to do, isn't it, if I want to be a man's man? You don't want the truth. You don't want to hear how my two best mates fucked my first love and made it nearly as hard for me to form friendships afterwards as to trust lovers, do you?

Well, tough. I'm in a confessional mood. We'll call my mates Mick and Steve, because if I'd been working class I might well have had mates called that. Instead of going to Oxford and meeting this pair of girlfriend-fucking country public schoolboy fops. And we'll call her Doris, because she's still my friend, and I loved her, and she would have made a good doris. If not for Mick and Steve.

It was my last year at university. After two years in college you had to live out. Me and Mick and Steve had got to know each other over the last few terms and while I had closer friends than them, people I'd known in London for years, they didn't want to live with me (because, like I'm going to show, mates are a bag of crap), so I lived with Mick and Steve, and also a bloke called Mark, who didn't fuck Doris, as far as I know, and was really called Mark.

I'll be honest. Doris and I had split up. But that still goes, doesn't it? Your doris is your doris as far as your mates are concerned, until you say otherwise. And Doris was mine.

I had spent most of my second year convinced that Doris was fucking either Mick or Steve. But when I asked our friends they told me not to be possessive, jealous and insane (three things I had always rather considered qualities than flaws). They all said: 'Look, she can't be fucking both of them, can she? So it's probably neither.'

I took them at their word. Moved in with Mick and Steve. Lived together. Cooked for each other. Went to the pub every night. Watched football. Even went to the '91 Cup Final with Steve and saw Gazza break his knee. Most of the time we got high and talked shite. Opened our little student hearts. But only in places.

Even when I steamed open letters to them in Doris's handwriting and found she had signed herself 'Honeybee' and 'Fluffymooch', I found ways to persuade myself it couldn't be. They just couldn't have moved in with me, knowing what they were doing, could they? Mates just don't. Mates, like the cliché says, are always there for you. Nothing else matters.

On my last night of college, before leaving forever, I was out having dinner with my new girlfriend, formerly a good friend of Doris's (do not talk to me about double standards – that is not what we are here for), and she just mentioned about Doris and Mick and Steve. I coughed or joked or vomited or something.

'I thought you knew,' she said. 'Everybody else knows.'

'But they all said she couldn't be fucking both of them, so if it wasn't both it probably wasn't either.'

'Yes, well, it was both,' she said. 'In fact for the last six months it's all been about how depressed Mick is that Doris has dumped him for Steve. Mick's distraught.'

My heart did not bleed for Mick. My heart bled for me.

For two years an entire town had been laughing at me because two of my mates, housemates even, had been shtumpfing my truelove. Ex-truelove. And so I asked myself: Who needs mates?

I wish I was a woman. Women have such nice friends. They

listen to each other. They try to understand each other. They empathise and weep for each other's woes. They talk honestly about sex. They do not, for example, lie to each other about how big their clitorises are or pretend to have lost their virginity when they were twelve to the au pair so as to make their friends feel small and miserable and childlike.

Mates, on the other hand, just talk. They don't listen, they don't care. They wait for you to finish talking so they can say something better. This is because men are boring. Men talk about football and beer. They are interested only in cars and tits and . . . no, just cars and tits.

Men compete. Men tell jokes to make themselves feel good, not to make you laugh. With mates you joust and spar and occasionally giggle at shallow things. You argue about ideology and international politics if you are educated, and about 5-4-1 if you're not. But the level of human interaction is the same. Women I have met three times know me better than men I've known since I was ten.

When things go wrong in your life you go out with your mates and you get wasted. You get wankered, you get fucked up, mullered, caned, cunted, schindlered, shrinered and shitfaced and then you have another drink and you think of more words for the only thing you ever do together. But you don't share feelings. And they don't give a toss, really. And then they fuck your truelove. Ex-truelove.

Whoever first said 'nothing else matters as long as you've got your mates' must truly have had nothing else at all.

Love in the Springtime

When Alfred Lord Tennyson in his poem, 'Locksley Hall' (1842), wrote that, 'In the spring a young man's fancy lightly turns to thoughts of love', he was widely believed.

It is a beautifully wrought phrase, full of vernal promise and altercating spondaic rhythms which, with its reliance upon pathetic fallacy, harks back, I would argue, to the values of the then recently defunct Romantic movement in poetry.

It is also utter bollocks.

When spring is in the air a young man's fancy does not lightly turn to thoughts of love, it turns – lightly or otherwise – to thoughts of rogering. It turns to thoughts of a couple of cool beers, a chat with a likely-looking bird you've only just noticed now that she's wearing a bit less, a brisk walk home together and a jab at the pink.

The problem for Tennyson back in 1842, however, was that: 'A young man's fancy lightly turns to thoughts of rogering' would not have rhymed with the line he had just written, which was: 'In the spring a livelier iris changes on the burnish'd dove' (and excuuuuuse me, Alfred, but just what on earth is *that* supposed to mean?).

And so he whacked down this steaming guff about love and knocked off for the day. No doubt to hurry down to the passport office to ask them why, exactly, they had put his title in between his first name and his last name, making him sound like some dufus American millionaire who'd bought the title online from the 'Toffs R Us' website, and didn't quite know where to put it.

I would like to set against Lord Tennyson's proposal the

counter-argument offered by Cole Porter 106 years later in his song 'Too Darn Hot', which was based, as he explains, on sound scientific evidence: 'According to the Kinsey Report/Every average man, you know,/Much prefers his lovey-dovey to court/ When the temperature is low/Cause when the thermometer goes way up/And the weather is sizzling hot/Mr. Pants for romance/A marine for his queen/A G.I. for his cutie-pie is not.'

Exactly. In the warmer months a man just wants bare naked shagging, not courting, not romance. It is in winter that one needs love. It is when the weather is cold that one needs the certainty of a warm woman to curl up with by the fire, to cook you a nice meal, to stroke your hair in the cinema – that is why men are generally faithful in winter. You don't want to risk a split up. You want to be able to get a bit fat, wear comfy old sweaters and know you are coming home to someone who will be happy to see you, no matter what.

But as soon as the first day of spring comes: Pow! Love is out the window and lust is in. And the first day of spring is, of course, Tit Monday.

Ahhh, Tit Monday. That glorious day in early spring when, heading into work on the bus, or walking to the Tube, or sitting on the train, you find yourself suddenly chirpier than you have been in months. You find yourself smiling again at strangers. There is a mild involuntary tumescence in your trousers that comes and goes throughout the morning with the comforting regularity of a heartbeat.

And then you get a text around lunchtime from a mate which says: 'At last, Tit Monday!' And you instantly understand why you are so happy. For Tit Monday is that special day in the year when, for the first time, the temperature rises above that magical point which causes girls getting dressed in the morning to decide to show a bit of skin.

After months of dull colours and chunky knits, the world's birds suddenly dive into last year's summer wardrobe (they have not yet had a chance to buy this season's stuff) and chuck it on without a thought. Your urban eyescape is suddenly lightened with acres of naked arm and leg and, after many dark months of burrowing, breasts rising again to the surface, like moles at dusk.

Big breasts in white work shirts, straining at the buttons. Small breasts braless in vest tops, the nipples frotted firm by ribby fabrics. Breasts in summer dresses bouncing in the distance so that they catch your eye before you even notice there is someone wearing them. Breasts nudging out from the crowd at traffic islands, quivering to cross the road . . .

And you know that it is nearly summer. For previous generations, the arrival of spring was heralded by the sound of the first cuckoo. For us, it is Tit Monday.

Not that it always falls on a Monday. Like Easter, Tit Monday is a movable feast. Last year, for example, it fell on a Friday. Friday 29 April, to be precise, when temperatures maxed out at 22.1 degrees Celsius after nothing much above 16 all year. It last fell on a Monday in 2007, when temperatures leapt to 22 on 24 April.

And then, of course, there is Tit Monday Night. You see, in early summer, temperatures drop off very dramatically when night falls (Tit Friday, 2009, dropped away to a parky 11.8). But the dollies are not prepared. Slightly stunned by the morning heat, they drag out the summer clothes but forget to bring a cardie (a mistake they will not make again until next year), so that when they're all standing outside All Bar One after work, celebrating the arrival of spring, their barely covered nipples have no protection from the cold. It's like a Bring-and-Buy sale where everyone has brought hat pegs. It's like a prog rock gig where, instead of lighters, everyone is holding up nipples.

So when will Tit Monday fall this year? Will you be the first to text your mates with the announcement? Do not shoot your bolt too early. There will be false starts. You will smell fresh-cut grass and see a couple of early starters and feel compelled to declare Tit Monday. But your more level-headed friends will tell you to hold your horses, keep your powder dry, do not fire until you see the whites of their bra straps. As the poet said: One bold northern slapper in a bikini top doth not a summer make.

Angry Restaurant Critics

I rarely choose to tell a story out of which I emerge looking like a complete arse. It's a writer's prerogative to tell what he wants to tell, and leave out what he prefers to be forgotten. But, hell, we're all friends here, and you know what a pillock I can sometimes be. So I'll tell it like it was.

My editor on *The Times* Magazine, Gill Morgan, was leaving the paper after 20 years and I had promised to take her out for lunch. I was foisted upon her at the end of 2001 for reasons lost in the mists of time and she had always been very tolerant of me. Always stood by me when I've made a tit of myself. Always given me a month off whenever the collapse of a patently unsuitable love affair meant that I could 'never write again'. So I couldn't take her to just any old place.

Unfortunately, in Wapping and its immediate environs even 'any old place' is quite a tough ask. Indeed, 'any old place', in the corrupted gastronomic language of Tower Hamlets, is tantamount to a hatful of Michelin stars anywhere else. Mostly there is nothing at all, and the places that there aren't are terrible.

But then I remembered that Roka had just opened in Canary Wharf, only three days by taxi from Times House. The original Roka in Charlotte Street is still going strong five years after getting one of the worst reviews I have ever given, so I thought this might be the time to say, 'Okay, you win', and try them again. Roka is famously plush, elegant and glitzy, after all, and thus ideal for a 'treat' lunch.

And I knew the food would be good. When I reviewed it in 2004 I was impressed by its then-fashionable pan-Asian-plus-sushi approach. It was the sort of stuff one found at Nobu, Sumosan and Zuma: Japanese for round-eyes. The great old cuisine made easy, accessible, cut down into little chunks and read aloud to children. Japanory, if you will. And they did it very well.

It was everything else that had upset me: the aggressive doormen, the snootiness, the craven mid-Noughties money-hunger, the screaming Eurotrashery. And I ripped it to shreds. And then, when everyone else loved it, was afraid to return.

But I'm told they've changed, and that the Canary Wharf outlet isn't like that at all. It could hardly afford to be, with a local catchment made up of lonely, under-salaried office wonks in polyester shirts taking a once-in-a-lifetime break from Prêt.

But I called ahead to smooth things, just in case. I don't normally do this. Normally, as you know, I go incognito in the quest for objectivity. But this wasn't about objectivity. This was about Gill. I wanted to make sure we would be welcome. I didn't want to risk, as happened in Charlotte Street, being looked up and down by a Transylvanian doorman and frogmarched into the basement for being poor. Nor did I want Gill to have to suffer a spit-flavoured Revenge Soup as part of her last hurrah.

With the call made, and the path smoothed, I called Gill to promise stacks of toro and rivers of Cristal, and said I'd pick her up on Friday at one. Which I did. And from the lowering shadow of the Wapping Fortress we headed out to Canary Wharf, staring out at the terrifying, dehumanised moonscape of Docklands from the back of the car like The Specials in the *Ghost Town* video, driving round and round that godforsaken, glass-walled circle of hell, goggling at the suited zombies and wondering if it could possibly be true that Roka was here at all.

'There it is!' cried Gill at last, many days since we had last sighted land. And so I paid the man his seven hundred pounds, and we bolted across the road and in.

The restaurant was humungous and rammed to the gills. Hundreds of people sat up at high, bar-like tables on three levels.

There was an open kitchen. Dozens of staff. Nobody greeted us. Nobody said 'Hi!' Nobody took our coats.

Typical, I thought to myself, and apologised to Gill. I grabbed a waitress, who told me to wait my turn. I waited and waited. I went to a till and buttonholed another waitress. She said there was no record of my reservation. She said they were full.

'Noooooooooooooooooooo!' I cried. This could not be. Not again. Not today.

I told her she MUST be wrong. That I had spoken with the boss. That I had SPECIFICALLY impressed upon them the importance of not screwing this up for me. She smiled. She was typical of Roka, I thought: jaw-droppingly beautiful and utterly useless. How could they have lost my reservation? MY reservation!

I asked for the manager. He couldn't help either. I said to Gill, 'I'm going to kill someone, I'm going to kill someone . . .'

The beautiful waitress said she'd try and find us a table. And while she tried, I had time to notice what an awful place it was. So loud and big and indelicate. So cheap-looking, so full of poorly dressed shlubs drinking pints and eating burgers. Burgers? What the HELL had Roka come to?

What a cynical exploitation of a name. How rudely misleading, to lure me out here, fully six thousand miles from home, on the basis of being Roka, and actually to be some cheapo diffusion knock-off money-spinning craphole imitation!

The beautiful girl showed us to a table. It was terrible! I refused it. Too near the loos. Too small. Too noisy. She said it was all they had. I telephoned Roka head office to threaten legal action, a TV exposé, mass death! But nobody answered. All out stabbing babies, no doubt.

Gill tried to calm me. She lifted me from the floor, where I was rolling and banging my fists and kicking my legs, and told the other terrified diners not to worry about my foaming mouth, it was quite normal.

'The table's fine, Giles,' she said. 'Let's just eat.'

They brought the menu and the wine list. They didn't have Cristal. They DIDN'T HAVE CRISTAL! Oh God. The Cristal was the only reason Gill had come! Roka was making a liar of me! By God I was going to slaughter them in print. Slaughter them!

I ordered a bottle of Dom Perignon, which was the best champagne they had, apologising all the while to Gill. As the waitress loosened the cage on the cork, I glanced down at the menu, at the salads and sandwiches, the potato wedges and pastas.

'Is the Japanese stuff on another menu?' I asked.

'Japanese?' said the waitress. 'We don't have Japanese food.'

I looked at Gill.

I looked down at the menu again, where it said 'The Parlour' at the top of the page.

'This. Is. Roka?' I said, as the cork popped open on the £135 bottle of Dom.

'No,' she said. 'This is The Parlour. Roka is upstairs.'

What else do you need to know? Do you need to hear about my hasty dropping of bank notes on the table and run for the door? About my effusive, grovelling apologies to the beautiful waitress, and her smiling refusals to take a tip from me?

Gill was beside herself. She just kept laughing all afternoon. When we did eventually find Roka, and sat down to a very good meal, I doubt she tasted a mouthful.

'I'm so glad you saved this experience for me!' she said, when she finally caught her breath. 'I'm so glad you saved your best till last.'

Acknowledgements

Most of these pieces originally appeared in one form or another in the pages of *The Times*. A small handful appeared in *GQ* (they are easily distinguished from the others by their increased sweariness). The respective editors of these publications, James Harding and Dylan Jones, put up no fight when I asked permission to reproduce my articles here. Indeed, they seemed only too pleased to be shot of them. I thank them warmly, just the same.

I would also like to thank the men and women who have edited me over the years. It has not been easy for them. I nudged my way into this business by developing a reputation for providing copy that was quick, cheap and just about useable. Little has changed. Except that I have become a bit more expensive, and more of a bastard. I am grateful to Graham Paterson for giving me my first writing jobs, to Michael Gove for giving me the opinion column which (at time of writing) I still have, and to Peter Stothard for giving me the *Times* restaurant gig. Then also to Gill Morgan, Tony Turnbull, Ben Preston, Anne Spackman, Robbie Millen, Danny Finkelstein and many others who could have fired me but didn't.

Despite appearances (and emails) I am most grateful of all to the sub-editors who have looked after my copy over the years. It has been horrid for them. I have particular reason to feel affection and gratitude to David Blundell, Fiona Gorman, Tim Rice, Paul Dunn, Christian Brook and Chris Riley. But a big thank you and a million apologies to all the others. I always thought I knew best, and, sometimes, it's true, I didn't. Although I can't specifically think of any actual examples . . .